Success on God's Terms

How to THINK, SPEAK and PERFORM to SEE the Kingdom of Heaven on Earth

by

C. THOMAS GAMBRELL
GERALD D. ROGERS

GRIP Media
PUBLISHING

Harlem ⎯⎯ Jacksonville

Cover Design by Michael Cox, Alpha Advertising, Sidell, IL

Photography by Shawn Wilson, ei8ht Studios, Jacksonville, Florida

Reach us on the Internet @ http://SuccessOnGodsTerms.com

Contents

—⟪⟫—

PART 1
Success on God's Terms: Core Principles

PART 2
The Creation Equation

PART 3
Occupy Until the Return

PART 4
Bonus Limited Deluxe Edition Content

Dedication

C. Thomas Gambrell

I dedicate this book to my family. God saw fit to connect us through blood, time, business, and/or spirit. I am grateful that I have had the opportunity to share the moments of my life on Earth with each of you. Your thoughts, words, and actions have helped to mold me into the man that I am this day. I look forward to what future days hold because God is not done with me yet.

A special dedication goes to the people mentioned below. Words cannot express the magnitude of my gratitude, so I will just write the following:

To my grandparents: Alma and Roscoe Gambrell and Jeffie Lee and Darbine Peacock, and my great-aunt, Ollie Blanchett—my inspirations

To my parents: Carlton Thomas Gambrell I and Eliza and Jerill M. Johnson—my first role models and my angel

To my co-author: Gerald D. Rogers—my Caleb

To Reverend Dr. Calvin O. Butts III, Bishop Wilbur L. Jones Sr., Bishop Carlton T. Brown, and Pastor Julia McMillan—my spiritual mentors

To David C. Allen—my business mentor

To my heirs: Gia, Maia, and Aaron—my reasons

Gerald D. Rogers

I dedicate this book to my loved ones who have inspired me to live a life of production and service. God has not given us the spirit of fear, and because of this understanding, the purpose of this book was born. This is just the beginning. The best is yet to come.

I give special gratitude and dedication to the following people. With limited words, I express sincere and heartfelt thankfulness, but I must list them:

To my grandmothers: Jeffie L. Peacock and Dorothy L. Frierson—thank you for my endurance

To my parents: James W. and Florence P. Rogers—I give you my unconditional love

To my wife: Maria "Chuck" Rogers—my cheerleader

To my children: Gerald II, Dyamond, and Azjaah—my joy and inspirations

To my granddaughter: Angel—my princess

To my coauthor: C. Thomas Gambrell—my Jonathan

To Traci: the beginning

To my spiritual parents: Bishop Vaughn and Lady Narlene McLaughlin—my hope

Acknowledgments

———◦◦◦———

With special thanks to Kenya Y. Wilson:
Thank you for your willingness to be the midwife for the birth of this book. Your heart of service has helped us deliver to the world that which God the Father through Christ Jesus has birthed through us. Thank you for the flawless transcription of the dozens of audio files from which this book was created. Thank you for editing the manuscript and providing us with the guidance we needed to get the job done. Thank you for your relentless effort and diligence, much gratitude. Without your hard work and professionalism, this book would not have been completed.

Our deepest gratitude goes to Robert L. Peacock, Sr.: Our uncle, our friend and a role model of all that is contained in this book. He is a mighty man of valor now living in the Kingdom of Heaven with God and Jesus. While on earth, he was an example of Success on God's Terms. He not only encouraged us to complete this project but he provided financial resources to ensure that it would be completed when the project came to a standstill. For that, we are eternally grateful.

C. Thomas Gambrell

To My Teacher Friends:
I once read a quote that stated, "There are no enemies or friends, only teachers." I am humbled by the fact that the people mentioned here have been my friends, and thus teachers, for many years. Thank you for the love, support, and mirrors of praise and correction. But thank you most of all for allowing God to use you to help build my character and personality. The cliché goes, "People

come into your life for a reason, season or a lifetime." I am so happy that you all are the exception to the rule, because in our case all three apply. You know the reasons, so I won't list them here and the season in my heart is a lifetime.

Thanks to: Dean A. Washington, Charisse Martinez, Debra Marcus Baboolall, Sharon Chappell, Tracie Lucas Lord, Terrence R. Woody, Walt F. J. Goodridge, Gary A. Ervin, Dr. Marian L. Gambrell, Andrew Morrison and Dr. Lynne Holden, Timothy and Rose Hall, Dr. Craig Bythewood, Jerome and Inocencia Chisolm, Derek Hawkins, Clifford L. Marshall, II, Toni Coleman Brown and Shanel Cooper-Sykes.

To Shamira Pongnon Howie: Thank you for the support and encouragement that helped me to stay focused as we completed this project. Thank you for your insight, feedback, contributions, prayers, and for challenging me to be precise in my delivery of the knowledge and information contained in this book. Our conversations, emails, text messages, and debates were valuable and timely. Thank you for shining your light in the valley on the dark days and on the mountain top when the clouds of adversity were nowhere to be found. My Sunshine!

Gerald D. Rogers

To C. Thomas Gambrell: Thanks for the opportunity to share our lives together. Thank you for blessing me and giving me the opportunity to serve with you shoulder to shoulder.

To Edmond M. Williams: Thank you for interrupting my life from the status quo and leading me to a place of true relationship with Christ.

To John W. Gray III: My brother and my friend, thank you for speaking through your prophetic voice. Now we have the manifestation.

To Alice Gray: Much love for allowing me to be transparent and ministering to my spirit in the true time of need and showing your unconditional love for me as your son.

To Steve and Tiffany Lloyd: The ultimate couple and the true epitome of unconditional friendship.

To Kelvin L. Pittman: Thank you for open arms and sharing your entrepreneurial genius.

To Traci L. Rogers-Battest: Thank you for creating a nurturing environment for our children.

To Bishop Mark McGuire: Thank you for relentless passion and sharing the gospel of Jesus Christ with power, sound doctrine, and conviction.

To Bishop Merton Clark: Thank you for your sense of compassion, sincerity, and depths of wisdom that you've freely given to me.

To Bishop Al Blue: Thank you for the impartation and the words spoken over 12 years ago that have now come to manifestation.

To Bishop Derek Calhoun: Thank you for your spirit of humility during our first encounter. Thank you for allowing your towel to supersede your title.

To Grayson B. Marshall: Thank you for the reprove and the rebuke and challenging me to a better me at all times.

To Keith and Pennie Williams: Thank you for your sincere prayers and unwavering support.

To James "Pop" and Elise Morgan: Thank you for truly accepting me as your own.

To Michael and Vivian Bradford: Thank you for your unwavering devotion for your grandchildren.

To Ben Goldsmith: Thank you for being a true prayer warrior and a man of faith.

To The Potter's House Christian Fellowship: Thank you for allowing me to serve you.

Prologue

Notes to Our Readers

"Commit your actions to the Lord, and your plans will succeed..."

Proverbs 16:3

C. Thomas Gambrell

Our mission is to galvanize a community of Christian business owners and success-minded people into accelerated Kingdom building activity, not only from a business or career standpoint, but also from an everyday living perspective. My coauthor, Gerald D. Rogers, and I are delighted by the fact that you are reading our book. We would like to start the dialogue and have this be a continuous process in order to bring the relevance of the Word of God to your activities outside of the brick-and-mortar church where you may be fellowshipping. Even if you're not attending church, these principles and laws still apply to your pursuit of success. This book is for everyone—there is no discrimination in the dissemination of the Word of God.

Over the past decade, operating as career-minded individuals, business owners, success coaches, and family men, we have gathered insight to share with you on how to achieve "good success" based on the spiritual laws found in the Christian Bible. This book is a manifestation of all of the trials, tribulations, and triumphs that we've had over the past ten years. With full hearts, we welcome you to *Success on God's Terms: How to Think, Speak and Perform to See the Kingdom of Heaven on Earth.*

So, dive right in and enjoy the learning experience. Thank you for taking this journey with us through the pages of our book.

Gerald D. Rogers

It is in a spirit of humility that we share with you the information found in this book. What we are sharing was given to us from our mentors and spiritual leaders. We're excited about the opportunity to help you develop into the person that you've been created and uniquely designed to be.

Remember, success is relative to where you are and there is no end point to the process. For you, reading this book may be the starting point or just a stepping stone on your journey. Nevertheless, we wish to catapult you along your path, in every facet of your life, so that you can have maximum impact in your local, regional, national, and international marketplaces.

Many individuals are looking for success, but we've realized through our studies and experiences that *success on God's terms* is the only type of success that is everlasting. We've designed this book to help you understand that, although material things are a part of success, the most important component is the character you possess. Only a character influenced by and grounded in the Word of God will allow you to have a lasting impact on the lives of the people in the communities you've been allowed to represent. These principles, if used properly, will allow your business to flourish in many arenas.

We challenge you to know where you are in your personal relationship with God through our Lord and Savior, Jesus the Christ. Utilize the information shared in these pages to maximize your earning potential in the marketplace, but more importantly, to be a witness and a living testament of the power of God.

We appreciate you for allowing us to serve you in this capacity. Thank you for your time, your energy, and your open heart.

Our Prayer for You

Father, we thank You for this moment in time. We pray, Lord, that You will continually guide and direct the paths of our readers and let this information be planted deeply in their hearts and have it return to You a thousand fold. Anoint their eyes to see clearly and open their hearts to receive the Spirit of the words on the pages that follow so that their minds and lives can be transformed. Let the words that they read speak to their souls. We thank You for this tool and mechanism to bring honor and glory to Your name. Thank You, for we declare these things in the name of Jesus. Amen.

How to Use this Book

The information in this book is not esoteric or something you have to contemplate for months, weeks, or years. We've been straightforward, transparent, and plain in our approach to designing this book. The idea behind this initiative is that we want to help you sift through the Word of God in a way that allows you to practically apply it to your daily life. Because the Word of God is plain and sure, we are all ministers—our lives are ministries to the people who are in our centers of influence. There is no gray area in our lives. We either lead people to the cross or away from it. Our life is our testimony. Either we're leading people to liberty and eternal life or we're leading them to destruction and certain death. You have to figure out what you want your life to reflect and determine the impact that you will have on people. If you're lukewarm in your role, you're leading people to death and destruction. If you have apathy and you're not vocal about the things that you see happening in and around you, the inactivity and silence leads people to destruction and death. It's like seeing someone standing in the street with their back to traffic and suddenly there's a truck driving towards them. You see the truck coming, but you don't say anything to the person and they wind up getting hit by the truck. The idea is that you have to be out there blasting and letting people know where you stand, if you are standing on the truth of the Word of God. That's all we want to model through this process.

Do your own study of the Bible verses at the beginning of each chapter. We would like to have a dialogue with you. The text for this project was taken from our sixteen-week *Success on God's Terms* teleseminar series. We have attempted to keep the dialogue in a conversational format as much as feasible. There is a premeditated flow to the topics, but each chapter stands on its own. Therefore, you can use the book as a reference guide and focus on the topic that resonates within you and you can read them in any order. We recommend browsing the chapters and pages on your first view, reading from the beginning to the end on your second pass, and studying each topic individually for a day or two, in any order you choose, on subsequent reads. Another great idea is to do the exercise above with a book club or Bible study group.

INTRODUCTION

————〜〜〜————

Faith of Our Mothers

". . .for you share the faith that first filled your grandmother Lois and your mother Eunice. And I know that same faith continues strong in you."

2 Timothy 1:5

*A*s we contemplated the structure and content of this book, it touched our hearts to begin our time with you by speaking about the people who planted the seeds of faith in us during our formative years. Before we knew God for ourselves, there were people standing in the gap for us and pointing us to the cross of Jesus. This book is fruit from the seeds of faith that were cultivated in us four decades ago. The simple message of this introduction is that we all have a role to play in each other's lives. Many people do not understand the power of prayer and the act of standing in the gap for someone in an intercessory manner. To illustrate this truth, we want to share with you brief stories of the inheritance left to us by our grandmothers and mothers—their faith...

C. Thomas Gambrell

For part of my formative years, I was raised by my maternal grandmother, Jeffie Lee Peacock. When I was living with her as a youth, I would watch her as she sat in her rocking chair reading and studying the Word of God. She would put on her glasses, get a pen, and then turn the pages, writing notes in the margin of her Bible. She introduced me to televangelists. I would watch the sermons on television with her as well as listen to them on the radio. This was in the mid-1970s, so some people were still listening to radio ministries as well as watching them on television. I was always intrigued by the fact that this was part of her daily routine. Those were early seeds that were planted within me. With all of the training that I've done, all of the reading and self-improvement, it was my grandmother who actually gave me the first book in that self-help arena, which was *The Power of Positive Thinking* by Norman Vincent Peale. She gave me that book when I was a teenager, but I didn't read it. The title just did not resonate with me at the time. A decade later, I read the book after I was instructed to do so by one of my mentors. When I saw the cover of the book, I remembered that my grandmother had given me the same book ten years earlier.

In addition to that, when I went from high school to college, she gave me a pocket Bible as a graduation gift. It is a leather-bound Bible and I still have it to this day. Wherever I am, that Bible is with me in my briefcase when I'm traveling and certainly in my possession when I'm at home. In that Bible, she placed a note with Scripture references on it as well as a list of words: *temperance, patience, insight, perseverance,* and *love.* She just marked the words down. There was not any dialogue before the words or after the words, no definition of the words, just a listing of words she felt would be important for me to know as I continued on my journey into manhood.

Not only was my mother's mother a God-fearing woman, but so was my father's mother, Alma Alice Gambrell. She took me to church when I was in her care. She was an usher for many years at the church she attended in Harlem, New York. So, these women really undergirded me in a way that allowed me to stand on their shoulders and on their faith. This brings to mind Paul speaking to Timothy in the third chapter of the second Book of Timothy, as the following passage illustrates:

"Timothy, I thank God for you—the God I serve with a clear conscience, just as my ancestors did. Night and day I constantly remember you in my prayers. I long to see you again, for I remember your tears as we parted. And I will be filled with joy when we are together again. I remember your genuine faith, for you share the faith that first filled your grandmother Lois and your mother Eunice. And I know that same faith continues strong in you. This is why I remind you to fan into flames the spiritual gift God gave you when I laid my hands on you. For God has not given us a spirit of fear and timidity, but of power, love, and self-discipline. So never be ashamed to tell others about our Lord. And don't be ashamed of me, either, even though I'm in prison for him. With the strength God gives you, be ready to suffer with me for the sake of the Good News. For God saved us and called us to live a holy life. He did this, not because we deserved it, but because that was his plan from before the beginning of time—to show us his grace through Christ Jesus. And now he has made all of this plain to us by the appearing of Christ Jesus, our Savior. He broke the power of death and illuminated the way to life and immortality through the Good News. And God chose me to be a preacher, an apostle, and a teacher of this Good News."
2 Timothy 1:3–11

I wanted you to read the Scripture above before I continued because there are a couple of key points in those verses. The first being that Paul acknowledges the fact that there was a spirit that communicated to Timothy through his mother and his grandmother. It was a fact that it existed in them first and it certainly had an influence on the life of Timothy as he took on the mantle of leadership as well as ministry under the mentorship of Paul. So, the first question that I ask you is what example are you setting for the people around you—the children and the adults? Are you leaving a bread-crumb trail to Jesus for them to follow as it relates to your faith? Paul talks to Timothy about believing, hoping, holding fast, and understanding that he was not given a spirit of fear, but of power, love, and self-discipline. As you study the Bible verses in this book's chapter, you'll find there is some very good meat in them with regard to the example of what we need to be—for those people who are in our center of influence.

In addition to my grandmothers, my mother was always an example and she is certainly my angel in the sense that we have been through thick and thin together. As I have grown into adolescence and young adulthood and eventual manhood, she has always been there for me. She wasn't the one to take me to church when I was a teenager. Instead of being in church a lot of Sundays, I was actually on baseball fields throughout the New York tri-state area. She worked tirelessly to put me through school and college and was always there as an example of the words her mother left in that note to me when she gave me the pocket Bible. I watched my mother live those principles before my eyes. So, although I wasn't truly saved until the age of 33, her example was there for me, the compass was set for me through the faith of my grandmothers and my mother.

My grandmothers have passed on to glory, but they left me an undeniable inheritance. They were not wealthy women from a financial standpoint, but they were filled with the Spirit of God and knowledge of God through Jesus the Christ. The inheritance that they left me was their faith. Beyond money, beyond material things, there's nothing more valuable. The following psalm was highlighted for me by my Grandma, Jeffie Lee. I share it with you now:

Psalm 19

"The heavens proclaim the glory of God. The skies display his craftsmanship. Day after day they continue to speak; night after night they make him known. They speak without a

sound or word; their voice is never heard. Yet their message has gone throughout the earth, and their words to all the world. God has made a home in the heavens for the sun. It bursts forth like a radiant bridegroom after his wedding. It rejoices like a great athlete eager to run the race. The sun rises at one end of the heavens and follows its course to the other end. Nothing can hide from its heat. The instructions of the Lord are perfect, reviving the soul. The decrees of the Lord are trustworthy, making wise the simple. The commandments of the Lord are right, bringing joy to the heart. The commands of the Lord are clear, giving insight for living. Reverence for the Lord is pure, lasting forever. The laws of the Lord are true; each one is fair. They are more desirable than gold, even the finest gold. They are sweeter than honey, even honey dripping from the comb. They are a warning to your servant, a great reward for those who obey them. How can I know all the sins lurking in my heart? Cleanse me from these hidden faults. Keep your servant from deliberate sins! Don't let them control me. Then I will be free of guilt and innocent of great sin. May the words of my mouth and the meditation of my heart be pleasing to you, O Lord, my rock and my redeemer."

I wanted you to read the text above for yourself. It was the first bit of Scripture my grandmother recommended that I read and study. This is the description of what God is to us. This is the inheritance my grandmother left for me from her faith, her belief, and her understanding that —even with all of the education I was going to get from the Ivy League institution that I attended, even with the money that I would be able to earn from being a graduate of that institution and pursuing my career in computer science and eventually entrepreneurship—if I didn't have God through Jesus Christ, then I really didn't have anything. She couldn't pay my tuition or contribute to my daily sustenance, but she gave me much more than any of those material things could ever possibly give. It is from the foundation of the faith seeds that these women sowed into my life that I have been able to reap my life's calling, as I have responded to the call of marketplace ministry and being a servant to all.

Gerald Rogers

I can remember, as a child, my grandmother encouraging me to read the Book of Psalms. She would also anoint my head with olive oil. At the time, I didn't have an understanding of what she was doing or preparing me for. It was not until I was presented with and accepted the Gospel of Jesus Christ that the significance of these events came to light. The seeds of her faith were planted in my heart and mind at an early age. Because of this, my heart was prepared to receive the Good News at the set time. I went from being a church member to having a true soul-saving encounter with the Lord in the twinkling of an eye, but the preparation for that moment took place over a couple of decades. That's really what *success on God's terms* is. When you've been regenerated and rebirthed in His likeness, you have the authority, power, and privilege to replicate yourself and be able to nurture others on their journey to the cross of Jesus. What God gives birth to never dies. He made the ultimate sacrifice by sending His Son, Jesus, into the earthly realm to pardon us from our sins—past, present, and future. Your success is tied into your willingness and ability to receive that sacrificial gift.

You're probably saying, *"What does my faith in God through Jesus have to do with the importance of having a strong foundation for my business life?"* What we're talking about when we speak of having *success on God's terms* is having the character of God in our personal life as well as our business endeavors. By doing that, we set ourselves in proper relationship with Him and that then allows us to have the proper relationship with people, clients, business associates, and employees. When we understand the dynamics of how we're to respond to people in our community, then we'll be able to have that same type of nurturing spirit that God gives us. God is male and female. He has the attributes of a man, but also a woman. The female gender has been uniquely designed to have a caregiving spirit. That's the same type of spirit that is necessary when it comes to developing and operating our businesses. In other words, you may have an idea that God has given you to build a business. Your idea usually starts out as a small seed. *Success on God's terms* wants to help you understand that this is a process you must be willing to endure from the beginning stages of your business growth and see it all the way through to the fruition of your dream in a way that empowers others dreams to come to fruition. Success is seldom immediate. You can expect your success to happen over a period of time. Nature gives us examples of this process all of the time. For instance, look at the process that it takes for a woman to bring a child into the world. In the natural, the gestation period for a human baby is nine months. From a sperm and an egg uniting, the infant starts out as a very small cell. The Scripture says we should never despise small beginnings. Starting from a single cell, it takes nine months of transformation for a fully formed infant to be birthed. The female, in most cases, is willing to make the ultimate sacrifice to bring the baby to full term. So, this is the parallel that we wish to illustrate. Just as a mother nourishes, protects, and cares for her unborn child, you must do the same for your business. It's going to take time, focus, and sacrifice for you to have *success on God's terms*, but the outcome is certain—a business that is a service to the community, a business that is profitable, and a business that perpetuates the *zoe* life of God.

Without a doubt, our grandmothers and mothers stood in the gap for us as it relates to our walk as modern-day disciples of Jesus. You must ultimately be the same type of vessel, to pour the Spirit of God into your business. Know that by thinking like God thinks, speaking like He speaks, and taking the proper actions as outlined in His Word, you'll ultimately see the manifestation of the vision of your enterprise. And because you've done it on His terms, this success will be perpetual and you'll leave a legacy that will far exceed the years that you'll be on this earth.

PART 1

Success on God's Terms: Core Principles

CHAPTER 1

—◦◦◦—

The Genesis of Success

"This Book of the Law shall not depart from your mouth, but you shall meditate in it day and night, that you may observe to do according to all that is written in it. For then you will make your way prosperous, and then you will have good success."

Joshua 1:8 NKJV

We begin our journey by expounding on the concept of the genesis of success. Adam was given a command in the garden. We find in Genesis, in the first chapter, that a simple command was given to us, along with the framework and everything that entailed our success on earth. It was all laid out for us by God. It was simple:

> *Then God blessed them, and God said to them, "Be fruitful and multiply; fill the earth and subdue it; have dominion over the fish of the sea, over the birds of the air, and over every living thing that moves on the earth. Genesis 1:28 NKJV*

So, the blueprint was already established for us to have dominion over all activity on earth. We must get back to our rightful place and facilitate true ownership, the way God intended it to be. We must replicate what exists in the Kingdom of Heaven right here on earth, where we've been ordained and purposed from birth to have dominion and to replenish. This simply means that we should be adding daily, not only increasing in our businesses, but also increasing in the family of God (Acts 2:47). There's a dual purpose here. We have the intent and the ability not only to dwell in the natural arena by acquiring land and wealth, but also to increase our spiritual families as well. That's been the mandate given and that's what we're excited about.

When people think about success, they often equate success with the accumulation of money and material things. Our equation for creating the type of success that we are speaking of is simple. To experience success the way God intended, we must think the thoughts of God, speak the Word of God, and perform the appropriate actions in order to see the outcomes that have been ordained. From the beginning of time, it was in the mind of God to give us success in our endeavors. He said, ". . .Let us make human beings in our image, to be like us. They will reign over the fish in the sea, the birds in the sky, the livestock, all the wild animals on the earth, and the small animals that scurry along the ground." (Genesis 1:26). We have been shaped and formed in His image. We, therefore, have the capacity to replicate many of His abilities here on earth. As He creates through thought and the vibration of His spoken Word, so can we. When we add performance and action to those powers, the only variable in the creation equation is time. Everything we want to manifest in our lives exists in our minds first. It's just a matter of us focusing our intention and attention on the matter long enough for it to actually materialize in a way that we are able to see the fruits of our labor.

Good Success versus Bad Success

One of the foundational Scriptures for our ministry is found in Joshua 1:8 (NKJV). It reads:

"This book of the law shall not depart from your mouth, but you shall meditate in it day and night, that you may observe to do according to all that is written in it. For then you will make your way prosperous, and then you will have good success. Have I not commanded you? Be strong and of good courage; do not be afraid, nor be dismayed, for the Lord your God is with you wherever you go." Joshua 1:8-9 NKJV

That is certainly something that we have to recognize. This commission was given to Joshua after the death of Moses. In this description, even though Joshua was Moses' minister, God proclaimed to Joshua that, if he would meditate day and night on this Word, he would have good success. So, it's not just about having success as the world views it. It is about having success that meets the requirements for good success as described in the Word of God. If there is success that is described as good, there must be a type of success that is in juxtaposition to what the Word of God proclaims. We want to make sure that we're on the right track to good success. We have to recognize that—as we've been talking about this whole concept of dominion and what it really means as it relates to being given the keys to the Kingdom of Heaven—in a sense, the formula has already been communicated for exactly what we need to do in order to perform in a way that will allow us to succeed in a good way. I think one of the things that has been a revelation for me is to realize that this is happening to me. I know that I was living under the ultimate deception of thinking that the devil or Satan had the power, but the idea is that he was allowed and *is* allowed to reign and rule over the earth based on God's Word and God's parameters. This doesn't mean he has to have control of you!

The ultimate goal is realizing or coming to the understanding that provision has been made for you and me to actually represent God on earth through the atonement and the process that Jesus experienced by going to Calvary, which represents His death, burial, and resurrection; and because He's been resurrected, everything has been restored to its initial state (John 3:16–17). We operate and understand that this is the beginning of our success because we've been reconciled to the dominion where we were placed, and we realize that out of our regeneration and our rebirth, receiving that gift now gives us the authority to operate and have dominion and rulership even according to Matthew 16:18–19, where Jesus said that *"the gates of hell shall not prevail against it"*—He's given us the keys to the Kingdom of Heaven. The keys, in this particular case, represent authority and give us the ability to operate. Being birthed into the right family now, we have the ability to restore, we have the ability to receive, we have the ability to go back and get everything that was taken away from us because no longer does the enemy have any power over any of us—once we accept the provision that was made for us through the cross at Calvary (Galatians 3:29). So, that's the Gospel, that's the Good News, and that's how you experience good success. That's how you experience *success on God's terms*, by submitting and receiving the regeneration through the death, burial, and resurrection of His Son, who made the ultimate sacrifice. This now allows us to represent as Ambassadors, to take dominion, to have rule and ownership of every economic system, every financial system, every educational system, and every media system. That's really the purpose we've been empowered and equipped to move in, because all of these things were established on our behalf.

Kingdom, Occupation, and Dominion

When we're talking about the Kingdom of Heaven, we're talking about a family that has already been established, and that simply means, because you've been birthed into the right family, you're entitled to all the privileges that come with being born into the right family. If you're thinking in the natural sense, you could be thinking about the King or Queen of England or other earthly royalty. Literally, the entire rule and authority has been given to them, not because of anything they did, but because they were simply born into the right family. So, being adopted into the Kingdom of God, that's something that you should be extremely excited about because, once you experience what took place on Calvary and accept it, you're washed by the blood and put in a position to have all the rights and privileges that come with being birthed into the right family. The occupation is simple as an Ambassador. We represent the Kingdom of Heaven, which has already been established by God. Now you understand the words, "Thy kingdom come, Thy will be done on earth as it is in heaven" (Matthew 6:10 KJV). We've actually aligned ourselves because we are now dual citizens. We have the right to command everything that's contrary to what the Kingdom stands for and access to the rights and privileges of being birthed into the right family. Anything that is out of divine order, we have the right and the authority to command to line up with the Word of God. Then, having dominion means we have total ownership of the rule of earth realizing as we come to a conscious level of understanding of who and what we are and to whom we belong—that it is our natural *right*, to have dominion over every aspect of our lives. Anything we come in contact with should, in God's time, yield or adhere to our commands. That's having dominion, and it goes back to the initial state where everything was intended and purposed. We're just reconnecting with our spiritual birthright by being born into the right family. As heirs of the King, we are Kingdom kids, birthed into the right family. We have rights and privileges that people who are outside of the Kingdom consciously and unconsciously don't have.

Then, there is occupying. We have the occupation of being Ambassadors, which means we should represent the Kingdom of God our Father wherever we are. We've been partnered in every aspect of our work and social environments. That's the command and respect that we must have and then we will simply acquire dominion because it's already been given to us. We've been given the keys to the Kingdom of Heaven and earth. This gives us total authority, total rule, and total authorship of how the story should end.

We want to make sure you have an opportunity to apply these principles, and not just to apply them to yourselves, but to share these principles with the people in your center of influence, bringing them to a conscious level of understanding about the privileges and rights that they have as children of God the Father and co-heirs with Jesus.

CHAPTER 2

—⟨⟨⟨○⟩⟩⟩—

Marketplace Ministry

"And he called his ten servants, and delivered them ten pounds, and said unto them, occupy till I come."

Luke 19:13 KJV

People are often curious about what we mean when we describe ourselves as marketplace ministers. Whether you're a business owner or an employee, we all have a role to play in the marketplace. The core concept of our message is marketplace ministry. According to Luke 19:13, we are to occupy or do business in the workplace until the return of Jesus. This is what we have been equipped to do. Once we receive Jesus, we all have a new purpose. This purpose is demonstrated by what takes place after the benediction, after we leave our local congregation. In essence, we're supposed to have dominion over every aspect of human life (Genesis 1:28), whether it's in the political arena, whether it's in the educational system, whether it's in the entertainment industry, or in the banking industry. We've literally been empowered and equipped to set the tone and affect every aspect of daily living. It comes down to the Scripture where Jesus declared that He came that we may have life and have it more abundantly. Therefore, everything that God intended for Adam and Eve to have in the garden of Eden, we are the Ambassadors of—for the Kingdom of God—charged with the responsibility to bring it all to fruition. All of creation is waiting on us to take hold of the mantle of our birthright as sons and daughters of God the Father and establish His Kingdom here on earth. Even in your communities, where you may see dilapidated buildings, that place is waiting for you to show up, for you to minister, to serve, and bring life back to that particular portion of the community. In your workplace, there are people that you're supposed to impact and affect, as well as in your social and recreational environments. Wherever you find yourself, that is your marketplace. Anything that takes place outside the four walls of your congregation, you're supposed to immediately start working on to bring life to it. That's our mandate, our mission, and we believe that we've been empowered and equipped to bring certain truths to the table—truths that will allow you to realize and experience with us the Kingdom of Heaven on earth.

eLife Ministry

We are doing our part by taking our mission to the marketplace under the banner of eLife Ministry. eLife Ministry is a virtual team of Christian lay ministers who are committed to assisting all people with the development of praise, prayer, and practical living skills that will prepare them to be faithful stewards of their time, talent, and treasure to the glory of God through Jesus the Christ. eLife is everyday, electronic, and eternal. We have engaged in different business activities in order to distribute the Word of God through a multimedia strategy. We have projects that will allow us, not only to have local, regional, and national impact, but we also have global initiatives planned.

GRIP Media Publishing is the publishing entity that produces all forms of media as they relate to bringing forth God's Word. GRIP is an acronym for God's Revelation in Print. We are producing books, digital content, online learning modules as well as eLearning simulations. *Success on God's Terms* is our initial branded book series. The first title, of course, is the book you are currently reading: *How to*

Think, Speak, and Perform to See the Kingdom of Heaven on Earth. We have contracted and will be working with ministers, pastors, subject matter experts, and other lay ministers to develop additional titles in the series to publish information about *success on God's terms* as it relates to finances, parenting, courting and marriage, to name just a few of the interesting topics we will address.

We've also established 12StonesEd.org, which is an online Christian educational training portal. We will be promoting this particular website as an eLearning platform, not only for the work that we'll be doing, but for creating private label versions of our 12StonesEd.org learning centers for church-based Christian education departments in order to support them in their missions. We believe 12StonesEd.org is something that's going to be tremendous as we work on helping the Word of God go forth by having the eLife Ministry platform of offerings as part of the core curriculum of all of our private-label learning centers.

We've also incorporated a recording label, Flint Head Records (http://FlintHeadRecords.com). Our first project, *Light, Salt, and Fire* is a hip-hop gospel CD plus curriculum for youth and young adults. This is part of our youth ministry and our initiative to put the Word of God in a digestible format for our young people by using the type of music that they listen to—the type of music that catches their attention. We are putting forth the Word in songs and working with ministers, pastors, and youth pastors across the country to customize appropriate curricula that will actually be tied to the CDs and DVDs that are published by the label.

Picture this on the canvas of your mind: The eLife Ministry team comes to your place of fellowship on a Friday evening and sponsors a concert for the youth of your community. Then, on Saturday, we return to deliver a series of seminars based on the curriculum tied to the songs that were performed the previous evening. It makes it possible for the event participants to be able to practically live every day with the Word of God by putting it in a form that is entertaining and nonconfrontational, as well as in a way that they can relate to and understand.

Next, we have our health and wellness ministry, GO TEAM Worldwide, HealTHY People Health and Wellness Campaign (http://GOTEAMWorldWide.com), which gives us a very well-rounded approach to health. We're partnering with nonprofit organizations, as well as entities that are in the health and wellness industry in order to promote whole wellbeing. This gives us a holistic 360 degree outlook into health and wellness from a spiritual, emotional, intellectual, financial, and physical standpoint.

As part our 10th Anniversary year-long celebration, we are giving away $10 million worth of business success coaching (http://BusinessCoachingGiveaway.com). God has put this on our hearts to empower believers, as well as those who are not believers in God through Christ Jesus all across the country and the globe. We're doing our part to stimulate the global economy. What this equates to is that we will coach 2,000 entrepreneurs on a nine-month program that will be housed within our 12StonesEd.org learning portal. Our goal is to help those individuals generate $100,000 in revenue as a result of our coaching. So, through their nine months in the coaching program, they will receive business success and personal development coaching valued at $600 per month—and this will be for each person. This equates to a little over $10 million worth of business coaching that we will give away. When you do the math, this equates to the production of $200,000,000 in revenue into the global economy as we help those 2,000 entrepreneurs create businesses that can produce revenues of $100,000 or more. This is our mission and what we've been called to do. We're answering the call of God to use our gifts and talents to establish His Kingdom here on earth and we're very serious about what we're doing. We're following a simple process of dictates and commands that He has set forth in His Word.

Other projects that are in development are a social network for Christians called the FellowshipoftheFlame.com and a private label bottled water ministry under the brand name Dry Land Springs. See the resource section of this book for more information on the initiatives mentioned above.

CHAPTER 3

—⋘⋙—

Hearing with the Ear in Your hEARt

"So be sure to pay attention to what you hear. To those who are open to my teaching, more understanding will be given. But to those who are not listening, even what they think they have will be taken away from them."

Luke 8:18

As success coaches, we have found, when developing a business, there are usually two things at the root of all successes or failures and they are *communication* and *planning*. We're not going to be talking about planning in this particular conversation. What we're focusing on is one of the elements of communication, which is listening. We want to share with you this topic of sound principles with regard to the concept of hearing and understanding with your heart versus merely listening with your ears. You're not only listening, but listening in a way that you can actually hear—a way that will help with the understanding of the words being communicated. You have to stop and think about what's being communicated and what *isn't* being said and what the nature of the words are in context to the conversation. In order to do this effectively, you have to actively use all three of your ears. Notice above that a little clue was given as to where your third ear is. We're all given two ears that are attached to the sides of our head, one on the left side and the other on the right side. I'm not talking about listening with these ears, but really hearing with your third ear. If you look at the word *heart*, the first four letters are h–e–a–r, the word *hear*, which I find very interesting. I'm not sure if that's a coincidence or not. Then, if you look at what's at the center of word *heart*, there are the three letters e–a–r. There you will find your third ear.

I was talking to one of my mentors and he was speaking to me about my heart. He said, "*C. Thomas, you were given two ears, but you have to begin to hear with your heart. There's an ear in your heart.*"

Now, picture me looking at him like he had three heads as he's talking to me about this third ear in my heart because I'm thinking to myself, "*Certainly, there's no ear inside the heart that is beating in my chest.*" But as he sat with me and he took out a piece of paper, he wrote out what I just described to you above regarding the word *heart*. What he said in closing his conversation with me was, "*When you hear with the ear in your heart, you can hear the person to a T*". I thought that was a very clever play on the word *heart* and really broke down the last letter of the word *heart* being "T". He began to talk to me in terms that I really didn't understand, but as I began to study and learn and deal with people more through my experiences, I really began to understand what he was saying.

Ignorant People

One of the things he was saying to me was that in our society there are a lot of clichés. There's also a lot of misinformation in society perpetuated by ignorant people. Now, the word *ignorant* is not meant to be offensive—it's just a way of describing someone who doesn't know. We're all ignorant of something. Everyone who will read this book is ignorant of something and whether you know you're ignorant or not, is irrelevant. There are certain things that we don't know about and there's no way for us to understand it because we're not even aware of the fact that we don't know about it—right? So, ignorance is not necessarily a negative thing. This was one of the things that my mentor talked about relating to this whole concept of hearing.

Feel with Your Mind; Think with Your Heart

My mentor said to me, *"I want you to think about what I'm saying. Don't make any judgments, just think about what I'm saying."* He went on to describe the fact that we're taught by society that we think with our minds. When you think about your brain, all of your senses are attached to it through your skin, nose, mouth, eyes, and ears. You have feeling in your skin, the nose smells, you taste through your mouth, have sight through your eyes, and your ears hear. So, all of those things are really connected to your brain and, without these things, we would have no way to interpret the world outside of our bodies. So,what he began to describe to me was this scenario where we really feel with our mind. Then he went on to talk about my heart. He said, *"Your heart has an ear in it and it's really the ear made for understanding. It's there to process information that you're getting from the environment. That information goes through your brain and it's processed in your heart. When your heart is hardened, information can't get into it because of hurt, fear, or those things that block positive energy."*

We know that when the children of Israel were fleeing Egypt, there were several references to God hardening Pharaoh's heart before he allowed the Hebrews to leave. Pharaoh's judgment became flawed once again as he pursued them. Because of that hardened heart, the Egyptians wound up in the sea while the children of Israel walked through it to the other side on to dry land. Yet, it was God who hardened Pharaoh's heart and caused his perception to be off.

It's your heart that determines the actions you take based on the information being fed into it. When people say unpleasant things to you and when you're seeing your bank account going up and down and your children are acting up, the state of your heart will determine the actions that you take in response to what you are experiencing. If your heart is distracted or hardened, calloused, or if it's been wounded or is filled with fear, then it's not going to respond the way that God would like for it to. When we allow the Word of God to occupy and sit on the throne of our heart, chances are greatly increased that we will respond with the appropriate action sanctioned by the Word of God.

Matters of the Heart

I want you to turn with me to Matthew, chapter 13. I want to give you an illustration through the words of Christ Jesus about this whole concept of understanding with your heart and that concept of hearing in a dual process that includes the ears on your head as well as the one in your heart. So, chapter 13 is the parable of the sower and, if you go to verse 9, it says, *"He who has an ear, let him hear."* I'm going to read through to verse 17 and then I'm going to backtrack to the beginning of the chapter just to make some references and to pull this all together. This is from the NIV version of the Bible and it says:

"Whoever has ears, let them hear." The disciples came to him and asked, "Why do you speak to the people in parables?" He replied, "Because the knowledge of the secrets of the kingdom of heaven has been given to you, but not to them. Whoever has will be given more, and they will have an abundance. Whoever does not have, even what they have will be taken from them. This is why I speak to them in parables: "Though seeing, they do not see; though hearing, they do not hear or understand. In them is fulfilled the prophecy of Isaiah: "You will be ever hearing but never understanding; you will be

ever seeing but never perceiving. For this people's heart has become calloused; they hardly hear with their ears, and they have closed their eyes. Otherwise they might see with their eyes, hear with their ears, understand with their hearts and turn, and I would heal them."

That reference refers to repentance.

"But blessed are your eyes because they see, and your ears because they hear. For truly I tell you, many prophets and righteous people longed to see what you see but did not see it, and to hear what you hear but did not hear it."

In the rest of that chapter, Jesus goes on to give the true meaning of the parable of the sower, but He also tells several other parables, such as the parable of The Mustard Seed, the parable of The Leaven, the parable of The Sower is explained, the parable of The Pearl of Great Price, and the parable of The Dragnet. This chapter really speaks to hearing, not just hearing with your ears, but understanding what you hear in your heart. Look at verse 13, which reads:

"This is why I speak to them in parables: 'Though seeing, they do not see; though hearing, they do not hear or understand."

So, that's a dual process with regard to hearing and, if you jump to verse 15, it says, *"Otherwise they might see with their eyes, hear with their ears, and understand with their hearts."* So, it's the ear in your heart that really gives you the understanding that you need to interpret what's being heard.

The filter of your heart is what sound goes through to process the words that someone else is speaking. So, if your heart is in the right place and lined up with the Word of God, it doesn't matter what people are saying or what you're hearing with your physical ears because it's going to be processed properly in your heart, where the Word of God resides, as you study and show yourself approved. Now, you have the thoughts of God inside of you. We've been talking about *success on God's terms* and you've heard the Word of God, so now when you speak something, not only are you speaking it from your thoughts, it's also being reinforced through your ears. So, you think it, you speak it, and then you hear it. Your words are not only going forth, but they're also coming back to you through your ears as you're speaking. As you take action, you can begin to see the fruit of your labor through the words you are speaking from your heart.

The State of Your Heart

When you have these external forces driving you on, the state of your heart is going to determine the actions that you take as a result of what you've been hearing. If you're full of fear, like those people who are talking about the recession and the possible collapse of the economy or the ones worried about hurricanes, earthquakes, or snow in southern climates and this being the end of the world, you will never make it. However, if you have the Word of God planted inside of you, you don't feel any trepidation because He already talks about these things in His Word. He talks about being in His presence. There should be no trepidation in what someone is saying as it relates to the economy if your heart is grounded the right way. If your heart is not grounded in the Word of God and is full of fear or hardened and nothing can get into it, then you won't have the ability to take the appropriate actions and turn so you can be healed. You won't be able to turn and find the prosperity that you're looking for or have the ability to repair a relationship that has collapsed.

Turning is all based on the state of your heart. The way you hear with your heart is by allowing the ear that's in your heart to be filled with compassion. You have to have the fruit of love and of the Spirit that the Word talks about inside of you. It's not just a thought process as it relates to the way that your brain operates and stores information, but it's the way your heart draws from those things that are stored in your memories. Your brain collects this information from your environment. You process information with your brain and store it in there. The condition of your heart should always be of concern to you. Have you been hurt in a way that has you stuck in that place in time, even though it happened many years ago? Have you matured at all? Did you learn anything from that experience? Are you playing that scenario over and over and over again in your mind and find that you're still stuck in the past, versus living in the current day because the state of your heart won't allow you to move forward?

You have to be in a position where you can hear with your heart. When you have the Word of God resonating on the inside of you, you have an opportunity to line up with Him so that you can be healed from whatever's ailing you. Can you take the appropriate action as you process the information in your mind that you're hearing with your ears? Are you listening with compassion? Are you listening with concern? Or are you listening just so you can give a response or reaction based on a hard heart, a hurting heart, one that's fearful, cowardly, cold, malicious, conniving, or manipulative? How are you approaching the world? If any negative things reside in your heart, you have to recognize that your hearing is a two-part process. Hearing is the physical process of sound waves created by things that are being communicated and those sound waves end up residing in your third ear, which is your heart, where every little thing is being processed through the *state* of your heart.

Imagination in the Heart

Turn to Genesis 8:21. I'm going to close out with this reference just to illustrate what I'm talking about and you can do your own study. If we go to chapter 8, verse 21 in the NIV version of the Bible it reads:

> *"The Lord smelled the pleasing aroma and said in his heart: 'Never again will I curse the ground because of man, even though every inclination of his heart is evil from childhood. And never again will I destroy all living creatures, as I have done.'"*

This was the promise that He made to Noah after the flood. He's saying that, from our childhood the inclination—and the King James Version says imagination, *". . .the imagination of his heart is evil from childhood. And never again will I destroy all living creatures."* We've all been taught that our imagination is in our mind. Here, clearly the Word of God talks about our imagination residing in our heart.

So, you have to really think about this whole concept. Do you really think with your mind or do you process the environment around you with your mind? As you feed your heart the Word of God, then that Word is there to be referenced and used as a filter. Everything that enters into your being can be filtered through the Word that resides in your heart and that's really the ear that you want to be able to understand with. Don't just hear what's being said, you want that Word being spoken to you, which is always life-giving, even when what's being spoken to you is ill-willed. You want it to be processed through your heart, that ear in your heart, so that you can hear to a "T." Only the Word of God can assist you with that. As you are presented with the opportunity to allow the Word of God to reside in your heart and be the controller who sits on the throne of your heart, God can heal you from anything. There's not a thing that He cannot heal you from or prepare you for as you allow your heart to be inhabited by the Word of God, the thoughts of God and the emotions of God through Jesus.

What's in Your Heart—Gerald Rogers' Testimony

As I began to wrap my mind around the understanding of how important it is to make sure your heart is properly aligned, I have come to realize that there's no way you can be successful in business, serve in your community or with the individuals you've been partnering with, unless you have your heart cleansed and purged from all setbacks, dilemmas, and struggles.

After doing research on this matter, I found myself beginning to understand the importance of how Jesus declared that *". . .man should not live by bread alone, but by every word the proceeds out of the mouth of God."* I realized that our whole being is based on what's in our hearts. As I was looking at the definition of the heart itself, some experts and scholars indicate that the human heart is considered as the center of our emotions and our personality, attributes of our inner-most thoughts and feelings. I am beginning to understand, in looking at the Word of God, the magnitude of how important it is that you understand that you can't even function properly if you do not have the right words planted in your heart. Then, because there are times when your mind can't distinguish between what's real and what's not, it will respond based on the filters that you've planted in your heart and it's only going to respond based on where your emotional state and emotional being are at the time. David asks in Psalm 42 verse 11, *"Why am I discouraged? Why is my heart so sad?",* which means *"Heart, why are you so emotionally distraught."* We understand that we have the authority to change our state of being because we're thinking the proper thoughts, and as we speak the Word of God over our situations, we have the ability to bring our hearts into subjection.

I found out that we cannot possibly operate in the realm in which we've been called to if we're deficient by not having the Word of God planted and rooted within our hearts. As I began to understand that, I took a look at a couple of things. I've learned that the heart itself can also be considered the seat of desire, where every inclination of man is rooted by the decisions he makes, and those inclinations will be indicated by the heart. Depending on your disposition, your heart can be hardened, based for example on you allowing your past experiences to interfere with your present life. We consider these things to be strongholds, those emotional traumas and people who've hurt you in the past, and as you rely and lay in that place of existence, it becomes perpetual and now you're unable to excel beyond that hurt or pain to get past that experience. So, you continually live it over and over again because you've not taken the time out to have your heart regenerated. Since the heart can be regarded as the seat of your emotions, we should always remember the Scripture declares that,

"...The LORD our God is one LORD: And thou shalt love the LORD thy God with all thine heart, and with all thy soul, and with all thy might. And these words, which I command thee this day, shall be in thine heart:" Deuteronomy 6:4–6 KJV

That means our very existence, our very being and whole desire should be to honor and please Him, and by doing so, He will allow you and me to move in the manifestation of His being because our hearts are pure and bent toward Him. This allows Him to consume us with His presence and His goodness and when we do, guess what? All of our existence then reflects the glory and the manner in which we are able to see the manifestation of the Kingdom of Heaven right here on the earth.

We're excited to know that, as we look at our situations from the viewpoint of our businesses and move toward having success the way God intended it, we are to realize and understand that man always looks at the outward appearance, but God searches our hearts. If you are now failing in your business endeavors, it is simply because you have not had your heart regenerated. God loves us so much that He knows the things He has in store for us. If we're not ready to receive those things yet, there's some purging that needs to take place in our hearts before He releases certain blessings to us. So, I wanted to share that with you, so you won't be frustrated. I know when God gives us a vision and we see the end from the beginning, during the purging process, there are some things that must be cut away before He allows us to receive the end results. He will circumcise our hearts and cut away those things that are not necessary or productive in our lives. The reason God does this can be found in (Proverbs 23:7 NKJV), where it simply says this, *"For as he thinks in his heart, so [is] he."* Here we go, back to the very beginning of where we started out. Our thought processes and our emotional state reside in our heart, but if we don't have the proper words to put in our mind to filter our hearts, then we'll never be able to see how the existence to which God has called us can be almost overwhelmingly wonderful. In understanding this, I know I'm blessed and honored to realize that the Word of God declares in Jeremiah 3:15, *"And I will give you shepherds after my own heart, who will guide you with knowledge and understanding."* God will assemble and place people in our lives who have His heart, so the compassion that He shows toward us, the mercy and the grace that He extends to us, and the ability we exhibit to want to attend to the needs of others first occurs because He resides in our hearts. He has a desire to have a personal relationship with each of us. His heart is to allow us to have right fellowship with Him, and because of that, He made the ultimate sacrifice. We're assured that in the last days, according to Jeremiah 3:15, He will give us pastors according to His heart, who will feed you and me with knowledge and understanding.

I want you to understand what is written in Jeremiah 29:11. This is the ultimate purpose and plan for manifestation when our hearts are properly aligned. So, we can be assured of this, according to Jeremiah 29:11–14, where He says,

"For I know the plans I have for you," says the LORD. "They are plans for good and not for disaster, to give you a future and a hope. In those days when you pray, I will listen. If you look for me wholeheartedly, you will find me. I will be found by you," says the LORD. "I will end your captivity and restore your fortunes. I will gather you out of the nations where I sent you and will bring you home again to your own land."

So, when our desire is to experience His presence and see His will manifested, we must search our hearts to be sure our motives are pure. Then, we can approach Him properly because the requests that we make unto Him are not filtered with self-consumption. It's all about being a blessing and being able to be of benefit to someone else from a business perspective. At this point, we've been able to lay our hearts open, cast our own selfish ambitions aside, and allow ourselves to be open for God's alignment to take place in us. Now, He can move into the areas of our deficiencies and our lack and surround us with His wisdom and bring us the resources necessary because our hearts are open and our motives are pure before Him.

So, we're excited to know that if we begin to understand that God loves us so much, that the heart may be the seat of our conscious and our moral character, then we'll continually bathe ourselves in the Word of God. As we find ourselves, what I have discovered in my own personal walk, is that I sometimes tend to look outward, but as I look at the Word, the Word of God is like a mirror, so it actually fills each of our hearts and individual dispositions. In James 4:2–3, it says,

> *"You want what you don't have, so you scheme and kill to get it. You are jealous of what others have, but you can't get it, so you fight and wage war to take it away from them. Yet you don't have what you want because you don't ask God for it. And even when you ask, you don't get it because your motives are all wrong—you want only what will give you pleasure."*

"So anytime we see ourselves petitioning or seeking things more than the will of God because of the condition of our hearts, it means that those things will not come into fruition and manifest themselves, because it's all about how our heart is positioned in that regard.

God will begin to circumcise and cut away the things that are unclean in our heart. He loves us so much that He is willing to show us how our heart can be pure. Then, because our hearts are pure, it makes it easy to obey and operate. Because of what He's promised us, obedience is better than sacrifice, and the only way we can truly work toward the manifestation of *success on God's terms* is to have an obedient heart, bent toward pleasing and doing the will of God the Father. Then, He can move on our behalf and take our *natural* and put His *super* on that *natural* and we have the manifestation of the same power that brought Christ Jesus from the dead. By spiritual birthright, it resides, works, and abides in you and me.

I want to leave you with the understanding that it's never what's on the outside of a man that defiles him, but what comes out of a man. What comes out of us is based on the condition of our heart. It's very important to read and understand this. So, I'll leave you with this from Matthew, chapter 15, verses 18–20,

> *"But the words you speak come from the heart—that's what defiles you. For from the heart come evil thoughts, murder, adultery, all sexual immorality, theft, lying, and slander. These are what defile you. . ."*

That's easy to understand and as we look at the situations we find oursleves in and the condition of our hearts, I will also read from the Book of Matthew, chapter 12, where He says in verses 33–37,

> *"A tree is identified by its fruit. If a tree is good, its fruit will be good. If a tree is bad, its fruit will be bad. You brood of snakes! How could evil men like you speak what is good and right? For whatever is in your heart determines what you say. A good person produces good things from the treasury of a*

good heart, and an evil person produces evil things from the
treasury of an evil heart. And I tell you this, you must give an
account on judgment day for every idle word you speak. The
words you say will either acquit you or condemn you."

At the end of the day, folks, being able to respond and listen with your third ear is going to be based on your emotional state. It's also going to be based on what type of sustenance you are getting, along with the Word that you feast on. It will indicate and dictate your speech patterns and your thought processes. In order for us to perform properly, speak properly, and think properly, our words have to line up with the Word of God and we have to walk with a clean and pure heart.

Sin Begins in the Heart

So, as in the psalm, David would say the heart's condition is going to be predicated on that thing which we tend not to want to deal with, that thing called sin. There's a remedy for that according to 1 John 1:9, where God says, *"But if we confess our sins to him, he is faithful and just to forgive us our sins and to cleanse us from all wickedness."* This will give us the purity of heart to operate and function in the manner in which we've been designed and called.

I pray that these words have challenged and encouraged you and, at the same time, helped you to understand that, regarding our success in business, if our hearts are pure, we'll never compromise our integrity. When we do business in the marketplace we've been assigned to, because we're acting in obedience, when God deals with us we're able to reflect and show compassion and mercy because our hearts are pure and bent toward serving His people. As a requirement of hearing with your third ear, there's a practical aspect that must take place and that's going to be rooted and grounded in how we submit to the voice of God.

CHAPTER 4

—⟨⟨⟨⟨⟨—

Submission

"Since we respected our earthly fathers who disciplined us, shouldn't we submit even more to the discipline of the Father of our spirits, and live forever?"

Hebrews 12:9

Disobedience

We're focused on this process as a blueprint to help people understand the power that they have access to from God through Jesus the Christ. That power is phenomenal, but the thing that stops the flow of this power in our lives, the power that God has made available to us, is this whole concept of disobedience. Disobedience can come about for many reasons. It might be because of ignorance or because no one has ever explained to the person what the power of God is all about. Perhaps they haven't heard the Gospel and they're just living their lives kind of willy-nilly and doing things that seem right to them. They could also in one way or another be going against the law that God has put in the universe. Disobedience is also prevalent in people who do know the Word of God and they're just going against it because they don't understand the repercussions of doing so. The reason they have not done certain things, many times, is because they have not submitted themselves to God. They have not submitted to the lordship of God the Father through Jesus as the model of how they should live. Nor paid particular attention to the example that God has given us in regard to being able to access the abundant power that He's made available to us as it pertains to our being created in His image. So, submission is a conscious decision. Parts of Scripture talk about being *transformed by the renewing of your mind.* As your mind is renewed, those thoughts that are set against God begin to come under subjection, but the thing that really gives you full power and full flow is submitting to the Word and the authority of God.

Submission is a weird word. Most people don't understand what it really means and they look at it as if it is something that makes you less-than or something that you do against your will. It seems to challenge the ego, but submission is just the acknowledgment of the divine power of God pressing us to do those things He has set as a blueprint in each of our lives, as a guide to how we should live our lives. It's outlined in Deuteronomy with the curses and the blessings. It's also outlined through the life of Jesus even before He physically appeared on the earth. Throughout the Old Testament, He is discussed in regard to the prophecies of the Messiah and the Anointed One that would come and set the captives free. It wasn't a physical bondage that He was coming to set us free from; it wasn't necessarily even a mental bondage, but was more so a spiritual bondage that we were in, based on the covenant that Adam broke in the garden of Eden as the first model of Christ. The first Adam was the Adam of the book of Genesis, and the second Adam was Christ Jesus in the physical form in which He manifested. So, in some ways, the concept of submission is a really tricky thing. The Scripture that many so-called Christians associate with the concept of submission is the following: "For wives, this means submit to your husbands as to the Lord." Ephesians 5:22.

The spirit of this sentence can be misleading if you take that verse of Scripture out of context. Some pastors have used this verse to subject woman to subserviency throughout history. When you couple that verse with the verse that proceeds it, you can see a different picture unfold and it becomes obvious that the sentence represents only part of what is being communicated in the chapter. Verse 21 reads "And further, submit to one another out of reverence for Christ."

It says "submit to one another." That means that husbands are to submit to the wives as well, if I'm reading that properly. You cannot separate those two verses and maintain the total meaning that is being conveyed. If you study the rest of that chapter, submission is outlined in full context. The rest of the chapter actually goes on to describe how the husband and wife are to submit to one another, but it also talks about the concept of this submission being a model. Submission in marriage is a model for the submission that needs to take place as it relates to submitting to God and how Jesus even submits to God and sacrificed Himself for the Church. When you read on in that chapter, it further explains submission between married couples and the relationship the concept has with the Body of Christ.

In a nutshell, the woman is to submit unconditional reverence for her husband and the man is to love his wife as Christ Jesus loved the Church, and ultimately died for the Church. The man is to submit unconditional love to the woman in order to put their relationship into its proper order. So, when the wife is submitting unconditional reverence for her husband and the husband submits unconditional love for his wife and is willing to die for her like Christ died for the Church, then that relationship is in harmony—because each person is getting what they need. The woman needs unconditional love and the man needs unconditional reverence. Of course, there's much more that goes into it, but as it's outlined in the Word of God, these are the things that we are to submit to in the marriage covenant. The main idea is that, when you study this chapter, the submission that He's talking about is not just from a physical standpoint, but also parallels the spiritual submission to God the Father. Even Jesus falls under submission to do the will of God. The example God gives us is one where we have to submit to Christ Jesus and, in doing so, we submit one to another as unto the Lord. When everyone properly submits, divine order is able to flourish in all relationships involved.

As divine order falls into alignment in relationships, the creative process that God has put in place allows you to flourish and live an abundant and affluent life, a life of prosperity. We're not just talking about money, but about peace and joy. Just imagine a situation where you don't have all the money you need. Maybe some of your physical needs are not met, but if you have peace in spite of that, it doesn't matter! When I think of that, I think of my maternal grandmother. My grandmother lived on public assistance most of my life, as well as on the money our parents, aunts, and uncles would send her until she made her transition to glory. Yet, this woman had peace beyond understanding and she never had a problem in regard to money. Money was not the significant part of her life because she had this peace and joy about her, based on her understanding of and her roots in the Word of God. The example that she modeled for me and my family members was a true testament to the fact that when you line up with divine order, the things in your life are also going to line up as God has ordained in the earth.

Everything is subject to order. There might seem to be a lot of chaos to us sometimes, with things that happen in the world from natural disasters to people hurting people, but there's a divine order to it all. God, through Jesus, is giving us an example of how to bring order into our lives. How do you turn chaos into order when you're feeling frustrated? If you have feelings of neglect, rejection, or any other negative thing, that is not the will of God for your life. Usually, when you're feeling those things, you're out of order. If your life is out of divine order, it can point back to one thing. So, you have to ask yourself, have you submitted wholeheartedly in mind, body, and soul to God? Have you truly submitted your body to God? Have you openly submitted your mind to God? Have you submitted your heart to God so that He might heal you? What about your finances? Have you submitted them to God? You want Him to put you in proper order and align you so you will be able to operate the way that you were designed to operate.

All Scripture has a reference. There are references throughout the Bible, with regard to the concept of submission. Not to overly complicate the matter, but you have to take your life and place it on the altar, as Abraham did with Isaac, as a testament to your belief and your faith in God with regard to your actions and thoughts. Before you take any action, are you representing the concept of "what would Jesus do"? Ask yourself, what would God have me do in this situation? Or are you going on impulse? Are you holding on to old thoughts around what your parents did to you when they were raising you and everything you're doing right now references those things they did to you versus what God has ordained in His Word for you? Or, are you despairing over something your spouse has done to you that really hurt you emotionally and scarred you, perhaps, even physically, and you're living in that past moment versus submitting those things to God and allowing Him to work in your personal situation as well as the situation that's outlined for you in His Word?

We have to really understand this whole concept of submission being key to your walk, not only from a spiritual standpoint, but also from the standpoint of you being able to build a business, a relationship or anything that you're looking to do in this life that involves other people. There is always some level of submission that you need to contemplate. A great reference point is submitting your thoughts and your actions unto the Lord. What would Jesus do? If you don't know what Christ would do because you haven't gotten into the Word, studied the Word, or read the Bible, you don't know the stories, the parables, or the lessons that have been taught, so more than likely, it's very difficult for you to operate from the context of "what would Jesus do". In order to recognize what Christ would do, you have to be knowledgeable of the things that He did while He was on this earth and understand the reasons that He came, that He died, and why He was resurrected. Above all, you must know the significance behind the shedding of His blood for the remission of our sins. He submitted every aspect of Himself to save us.

Just imagine a person dying on a cross, nailed to that cross, and taking on the sin of not only the past and current generations, but all future generations as well. What kind of price must that have been?

Think about someone taking on all sin, past, present, and future, once and for all. Think about Jesus being willing to die for us the way that He did, submitting to those things that He had possession of from a spiritual and physical standpoint. God honored that by raising Him up from the dead and because of that, He now sits at the right hand of His Father and intercedes for us constantly as we continue to sin, fall short, and repent. As we study and grow, we teach and learn. We mature as Christians, human beings, and spiritual beings. We are able to do this through submission. So, we must take all those things that we possess and be of the mind that we possess no thing and in possessing no thing, we can possess everything because we've submitted everything we have to the Lord. Our possessions, children, houses, parents, jobs, businesses, occupations, recreation, and every aspect of our being, we must submit to the Lord. As you recognize this as the way to live your life, God can do the healing work He has put in the hands of Jesus the Christ. He has given us the ability to submit to the lordship and the authority of His Son, Jesus, and now we can receive the blessings that come with that. If you find dissonance in your life or negative energy, you need to submit it unto the Lord and align yourselves with the Word, so that you can be transformed and can receive the blessings that He's laid out for us.

There's more that we could talk about, but my understanding is that the simplicity of the message usually makes the biggest point. The idea is that we must submit all that we possess to God and possess no thing, so that we can possess all things through Jesus, and those things that God has lined up for us.

Submission Defined

The word *submit* means "to give over or yield to the power or authority of another, to comply or to act, to be in accordance." It also means "to obey." That means you have to totally comply with, follow and agree. The word *yield* means "to yield, to give up as to superior power or authority, to surrender or submit as to superior power." So, when we look at the word *submission* from a business perspective, we find it to be the key in keeping order so we will be successful as we apply this from day to day.

First of all, in order for you to move forward, you have to be totally submitted to the will, thoughts, words, speech, action, and to the heart of God. By doing this, it will allow you to fuse yourself to Him and attract others. Remember, everything that we're sharing with you, we're sharing as it pertains to *success on God's terms*. His laws are irrefutable and this is simply about the law of reciprocity. So, we must be willing to submit as Jesus submitted to the death of the cross. Because He submitted to the death of the cross, He now reigns in Heaven. We have that same ability to submit as we follow the example that was set by our Lord and Saviour. Also, understand that submission simply means no matter where you are in life, whether you have had success or not, although you may be in authority, you're still under authority. You will always have those types of relationships, no matter what level of success you rise to, where you're under His authority. When you understand that, just remember that, ultimately, we're all submitted unto God. Yet, even in the physical, natural realm, there should always be someone that you're submitted to so that you never get beyond yourself—because the first opportunity you have to go against the physical authority that's been placed over you, it's going to disrupt the flow of how you navigate through your business, in your day-to-day activities, your personal relationships, and your business relationships. This is very important because as you're willing to submit to authority, when it's your turn to reign and rule, because you've sown, it's going to be easy for you to receive.

So, what are we talking about? We're talking about a couple of things here that I just want to highlight from a verse of Scripture. Let's explore what happens when you and I submit ourselves, first of all to God, and because we've submitted ourselves to Him by following His guidelines and rules and the way He would have us to perform, out of our obedience there are some wonderful things that take place. As you look at your business and where you are in life, everything should be spiritual first, then natural. Once we understand the spiritual concepts of how God operates, then we're talking about *success on God's terms* and we will be able to navigate through every aspect of the elevation from level to level, from business to business and relationship to relationship. I just want you to keep this in your hearing so you understand that the word *submit* is synonymous with *obey*, which simply means "to comply or follow." Now, here's the benefit of your submitting to God's authority and obeying His voice: the promise that you have tied to your obedience is caused by your submission and following His Word.

Deuteronomy 28:1–6 says this in The Message Bible:

> *"If you listen obediently to the voice of God, your God, and heartily obey all his commandments that I command you today, God, your God, will place you on high, high above all the nations of the world. All the blessings will come down on you and spread out beyond you because you have responded to the voice of God, your God."*

We're talking about simply submitting to the voice of God, and because you've submitted appropriately, this is what will happen—because God is not like man that He should lie, neither the son of Man, that He should repent. So, whatever God has spoken and promised you, it will come to pass based on your obedience, your submission to His will, and to His way. Here are the blessings that will result from your submitting to the voice and the Word of God. Deuteronomy 28:1–6 continues;

> *"God's blessing inside the city,* [No matter where you go, you will be blessed.] *God's blessing in the country; God's blessing on your children, the crops of your land,* [We're talking about

your business now.] the young of your livestock, the calves of your herds. [So, whatever business you have will flourish because you've submitted to the Word of God.] God's blessing on your basket and bread bowl; [Meaning you will never go hungry, that you will never be in lack.] *blessing in your coming in, and blessing in your going out."*

So, no matter where you go, no matter where you set up shop, no matter what city you're in, and regardless of what's going on around you, because you've submitted properly to the things and the voice of God, this promise will come to pass. Then, listen to this folks,

"God will defeat your enemies who attack you. They'll come at you on one road and run away on seven roads."
Deuteronomy 28:7 The Message

In other words, you may be seemingly unable to fight for yourselves and your circumstances or resources may not necessarily be there, but God will always make provision for you because of His Word.

"God will order a blessing on your barns and workplaces; he'll bless you in the land that God, your God, is giving you. God will form you as a people holy to him, just as he promised you, if you keep the commandments of God, your God, and live the way he has shown you. All the peoples on Earth will see you living under the name of God and hold you in respectful awe. God will lavish you with good things; children from your womb, offspring from your animals, and crops from your land, the land that God promised your ancestors that he would give you.

God will throw open the doors of his sky vaults and pour rain on your land on schedule and bless the work you take in hand. You will lend to many nations but you yourself won't have to take out a loan. God will make you the head, not the tail; you'll always be the top dog, never the bottom dog, as you obediently listen to and diligently keep the commands of God, your God, that I am commanding you today. Don't swerve an inch to the right or left from the words that I command you today by going off following and worshiping other gods." Deuteronomy 28:8–14 The Message

So, those are the promises we can look forward to when we submit our lives to God and we're obedient to His voice.

You should get really excited about understanding how to have *success on God's terms* simply by submitting and then remembering that, although you may be *in* authority and you may be a business owner, you're also *under* authority as well. Christ Jesus had the same responsibility, to submit to His Father in Heaven, but at the same time, He was *in* authority as He led the disciples to a better place and gave them understanding of the things of the Kingdom of Heaven. Have you submitted, first of all to God? Then, have you truly submitted to a mentor, someone who can guide and direct your path? You cannot possibly lead others if you haven't submitted yourself. As you submit yourself, guess what? It will open the door for you to have access to those who encourage and inspire you, so it creates a dual role. Just as we read, submitting one to another as unto the Lord allows us to reverence our Lord. Then, everything we do will replicate and duplicate.

We're talking about *success on God's terms* in its entirety. First of all, our thought processes, then our speech, then our actions, then our performance, then the manifestation because if our heart is right and our will is submitted, then by default we'll continue walking in blessings, which we've all been speaking of.

CHAPTER 5

——ฆฆ——

Prayer

"So this afternoon when I came to the spring I prayed this prayer:
'O LORD, the God of my master, Abraham, if you are planning to
make my mission a success, please guide me in a special way.'"

Genesis 24:42

When we look at *success on God's terms* and the concept of how to think, speak and perform to see the kingdom of Heaven on earth, there are some essentials that can never ever be excluded from your success, from a personal and business standpoint. There is an underlying theme in what we believe the Lord has placed on our hearts with regard to this book. Before we share this information, we're actually going to invoke the presence of God. We're going to seek Him right now, that He may dwell in your space as you read the text of this chapter.

Prayer

"Father God, we come before You humbly, understanding, first of all, that You've allowed us to partake in this process of transformation and You've allowed us to assemble at this place in time. Because You are so sovereign, we acknowledge the fact that, in and of ourselves, we can do nothing without You. So, we yield right now our will to Yours and we pray right now, Lord, that You would simply dwell in this atmosphere and on these lines, that our hearts will be ready to receive and Your purpose will be fulfilled in those who are reading. Allow there to be a true impartation that takes place as we continue to walk through this discussion of *success on God's terms*, where we think, speak, and perform to see the Kingdom of Heaven on earth according to Your purpose. So, we just say, *'Thank You'* right now. We appreciate You and we ask these things in Your Son, Jesus' name. Amen."

Types of Prayer

What is prayer? Is it a repetition of words? Is it something that we should do continually? The Word of God always admonishes us to seek Him and pray daily. As we invoke His presence and His will and get His perspective on things, then we will always end up making the right purposed decision because of His involvement. In understanding that our battles are His responsibility because we're operating not under our own power or might but under His, provides us the knowledge that He gives us the ability to impact and change lives. What type of prayer life do you have? What type of prayer language do you have? Are you in constant communication with God throughout the day? Because, as we think about our different concepts of who God is and what He's called us to, prayer is absolutely awesome. I'm going to give you some basic definitions and as you're reading these definitions, I want you to understand that communicating with God the Father through His Son, Christ Jesus, is simply about effective communication.

Prayer is a *devout petition to God*. It's a *spiritual commune with God in regard to supplication; thanksgiving; adoration* as well as *confession*. It's a *formula or sequence of words used in an appointed time for praying*. It's the *ability to have constant and continual communication, realizing it's a reverent petition made to God; the act of making a reverent petition to God.* Also, when thinking about prayer, we must understand that it's mandatory, a requirement we must practice in order to be able to download divine supernatural instruction, so that we will be able to deal with the things we have to deal with on a natural basis—as we come to comprehend that we are created spiritual beings, but our bodies are at constant enmity with one another, flesh, and spirit. Our whole understanding of our spiritual prayer life gives us the ability to deal with the experiences you may be dealing with in your personal realm as well as your business realm. So, we will always have the ability to take our natural and invoke the supernatural, which allows us to navigate through things, which the mind cannot conceivably understand. Prayer is a conversation with God, the intercourse of the soul with God, not in contemplation or meditation, but in direct address to Him. Prayer may be spoken out loud or whispered completely in the mind, occasionally or constantly. The more you seek Him, the more peace you will find in your situations. So, as you're thinking about what it means to seek the face of God, there are a couple of Scriptures that come to mind that I want to share with you, Scriptures that speak to the importance of understanding the significance of what prayer will do for you.

Let's read a verse of Scripture out of the King James Version of the Bible,

"And the prayer of faith shall save the sick, and the Lord shall raise him up; and if he have committed sins, they shall be forgiven him." James 5:15

As we petition the Lord in prayer, there are a couple of things we must do. First of all, in order to approach God properly, there are different types of prayer that we must recognize. Because God is a holy God, He says, *"Be ye holy, for I am holy,"* (Leviticus 11:45) so as we come to God, we must come confessing our sins, whether they're sins that we've obviously done or what we call sins of omission or commission. This means, before we even come into His presence, we need to make sure we're coming in a humble manner, asking or seeking forgiveness. This is the first type of prayer.

The second type of prayer now allows God to commune and fellowship with us. Because He is a holy God, if there is unconfessed sin in our lives, His ears are not necessarily open to move on our behalf. Here's what you have to understand: once we've confessed our sins and because of the covenant He's established with us, now He's obligated to move on our behalf. So, if you're walking around knowing there is unconfessed sins in your life, then Father God is not obligated to act on your behalf, but when you have right fellowship and commune with Him, you want to make that confession. Now, you're in a position and a place where He is obligated to move on your behalf.

The main type of prayer is a prayer of thanksgiving, being thankful for what He's already done. Sometimes when we get enamored with life's situations, we fail to just say *"Thank You."* When we say *"Thank You,"* we're saying we're thankful for the fact that we have the ability to speak to God personally, to utilize our limbs, to speak, to feed ourselves, that we're clothed, and in our right minds. We come to God with confessions of our sins and we understand the prayer of thanksgiving.

Then, we come with our prayer of adoration, just adoring the fact that He's given us the ability to act or He's acting on our behalf. He's fighting every battle for us. You fall into a prayer of adoration just by acknowledging the fact that, without Him, you couldn't accomplish anything. This is the basis of a prayer of adoration. Ultimately, a prayer of adoration leads to a prayer of worship.

When you understand the exquisite worthiness of God and that He does many of the things you've petitioned or asked of Him, even when you don't deserve it, it leads to a stance of open worship. We all know that we are sinners and fall short of His Glory, so the fact that he recognizes us is a true testament to His love for us. His omnipotent, omniscient, and omnipresent Glory is unfathomable to any of us, but He hears us and allows miracles, signs, and wonders to manifest in our lives, which increases our faith and our love for Him. We're never alone.

In many instances, He's already fulfilled your request before you acknowledge Him through worship. Through prayers of petition, when you simply seek the face of God and ask Him to do things on your behalf, He hears. You may be praying to the Lord to place people in your path who would enhance your business or you may ask the Lord to move financially on behalf of your business or in your personal life. These are prayers of petition. Yet, nothing happens until you've approached Him properly, first, confessing your sins to God. Secondly, you acknowledge by approaching Him from a realm of thanksgiving. Those are the things that are going to lead you and allow you to seek the face of God in making your prayer of petition. Then, because you've aligned yourself properly, the God of the universe is now obligated to act on your behalf because—here's what you've got to understand— because of the blood of Jesus, God has already stepped in for you and me, to intercede on our behalf. Now you have the privilege of seeking the face of God, but more importantly, because you've properly aligned yourself, you've allowed that He move on your behalf.

So, as you're thinking about prayer and how important it is, in Proverbs 8:17 KJV it says, "I love them that love me; and those that seek me early shall find me". God is a God who is omnipotent, meaning that He has all power; He's omniscient, He knows everything about you; He's omnipresent, so He's everywhere. Here's what a word of prayer does for you: as you petition Him early in the morning and allow Him to go before you to navigate your paths, making all the crooked places straight, putting people in your path who are going to be a conduit to fulfill a purpose in your life, because you have allowed Him to act on your behalf by properly petitioning and trusting in Him, He teaches you how to navigate your day. Then, the Word of God says in Proverbs 3 that we should:

"Trust in the LORD with all your heart; do not depend on your own understanding. In all thy ways acknowledge him, and he shall direct thy paths. Seek his will in all you do, and he will direct your paths." Proverbs 3:5–6

This is a supernatural agent because of the Spirit of God and the continual communication that you have with Him. What allows you and I to navigate and be able to operate in every aspect of our lives, whether it's business or personal, is our devotion to our prayer life. Then, because you continuously have this personal intimacy with God, you are able, not only to fellowship with Him, but to have the mind of God. You'll be able to take the actions of God as He leads you. Then, you'll also have the speech of God.

In the Word of God, He said in Genesis 1:26, "Let us make people in our image, to be like ourselves. They will be masters over all life. . ." This is where you have to understand the power of your voice. You now have the ability to operate and seek the face of God. When you get to this point, you will be given the ability to walk on that path and operate in the realm to which you've been called. As you petition the Lord on behalf of your business, according to the Word of God, *"If you commit your ways and thoughts unto Him, then shall He establish your path and establish your works."*

So, my question to you is: what does your prayer life look like? How often, how many times have you come before the God of the universe and allowed Him to speak to you? Are you listening?

Here's the other thing about prayer: After you've spoken, the part we all have difficulty with is listening for the response. As you verbalize your prayers, you must also meditate on what you're saying as you petition the Lord. There are instructions that will be given and the Word of God says,

"For my thoughts are not your thoughts, neither are your ways my ways, saith the LORD. For as the heavens are higher than the earth, so are my ways higher than your ways, and my thoughts than your thoughts." Isaiah 55:8–9 KJV

He gives you the perspective of a heavenly view dealing with an earthly situation. You're actually limiting yourself if you do not have a timely prayer life or if you do not take the time out to commune and fellowship with Him because that allows you the ability to navigate through your day with success. The Word of God says in Ephesians 3:20:

"Now glory be to God! By his mighty power at work within us, he is able to accomplish infinitely more than we would ever dare to ask or hope."

As you begin to have the mind of Jesus the Christ and understand the words of God, you'll be able to tap into a supernatural power that gives you the ability to far exceed any of the things that you've fathomed or even imagined. You do not have the capability to begin to think what God would do with you through your business and in your personal life. It all comes by starting with prayer.

There are a couple of other verses that I want to share with you here. Realizing that you've petitioned the Lord properly, you've taken time out to commune with Him; you've gotten instructions early in the day; your day begins with devoted time; and, you have the understanding that He's already carved you a way out of your problems. This is illustrated in Philippians 4:6–7, this is one of the verses I was able to personally tap into because it gave me peace no matter what financial situation I was facing, no matter what trouble I was experiencing on a personal level. Then, I began to meditate and understand these two things. Starting in Philippians 4:4–5 KJV, it says:

"Rejoice in the Lord always: and again I say rejoice. Let your moderation be known unto all men. The Lord is at hand."

In other words, He's acting, He's ready, and He's already positioned Himself to act on your behalf. It says:

> *"Be careful for nothing; but in everything by prayer and supplication with thanksgiving let your requests be made known unto to God. And the peace of God, which passeth all understanding, shall keep your hearts and minds through Christ Jesus."* Phillipians 4:6–7 KJV

The New Living Translation gives a deeper revelation of what this means.

> *"Always be full of joy in the Lord. I say again, rejoice. Let everyone see you are considerate in all you do. Remember the Lord is coming soon."* Philippians 4:4–5

Here's what I really want you to understand:

> *"Don't worry about anything. Instead, pray about everything. Tell God what you need and thank Him for all that He has done. Then you will experience God's peace, which exceeds anything we can understand. His peace will guard your hearts and minds as you live in Christ Jesus."* Phillipians 4:6–7

Folks, this is what prayer will do for you. Prayer is key. Understanding this dynamic, you can rest assured that, when you've petitioned the Lord properly and confessed your sins properly, God has made a promise to act on your behalf. You do not have to worry about anything. Instead of worrying about anything, pray about everything and cast all your cares on the Lord, knowing that He cares for you.

Then you'll find there's a peace that surpasses all understanding. Your life could be in total turmoil, your business could be falling apart, but because you realize you have an advocate who's continually making intercession on your behalf, knowing your cry unto the Lord, your petition unto Him moves forward and allows Heaven to act on your behalf. Because you are a child of God, you are His responsibility and He's obligated to defend your honor. It's not your reputation at stake, but His.

The Key to Prayer—The Silence that Follows

The key to prayer is having that personal relationship with God through Jesus, with Jesus as the mediator. You must develop the ability to get in God's presence in a premeditated fashion, not only to create a petition or to make a request, but to understand more about God through communing, conversing, and sending up prayers. One of the key parts of any prayer time is not only what's coming out of your mouth verbally, but the quiet that follows—or should follow—your prayer petition or your prayer of intercession. You should also have some quiet meditation as part of your prayer time, to hear from God and to receive from Him because He will speak to your spirit; He will talk to you in that prayer time, if you make provisions for it as part of your process. If you're always the one talking, always the one making a request and you don't provide the space for God to speak to you, then sometimes you may miss exactly what He has for you as an answer to your current or past prayer. I know in that meditative space after verbally making my petitions and my intercessions, I find this to be something that's very key as part of that prayer time. If you haven't incorporated that space of silence, then you should certainly make provisions to create that space so that you can hear from God. Prayer time is that personal communication, that personal relationship, and you want to make sure you create an environment that allows for two-way communication versus a one-way request or petition.

When we talk about *success on God's terms*, we're talking about your own intimate personal relationship with God the Father of the universe, so that deals with your vertical relationship. Our horizontal relationships deal with our daily interaction with the people in the communities that we serve. Amos 3:3 says, *"Can two people walk together without agreeing on the direction?"* So, as you're petitioning, it's important for you to understand there must be a two-way conversation between you and God, and this will save you a lot of trauma in regard to building a successful business. You're petitioning the Lord to help you, to improve you, empower and equip you to facilitate your business, so your prayer should be to have people who are like-minded and like-spirited to help you to develop and cultivate your business. I'm going to ask you, as you contemplate and digest this information, what type of people you're looking to do business with? If you set the foundation properly and seek the face of God to bring you business people to help you develop your business and put the right people in your path, because that prayer is continuously prayed, you can rest assured that you will have the discernment necessary to enter into covenant relationships with the right individuals.

This is the challenge we all have as aspiring business owners and entrepreneurs. Sometimes, we get too excited about the financial rewards of a short-term temporary transaction when we're looking to develop long-term businesses. We need to understand how to seek the right type of business relationships and the right type of business that we should be working with because it's going to be perpetual. This is the type of foundation that we want to have when it comes to building businesses. We want to be able to leave a legacy; we want to be able to set a precedent and a standard that won't be compromised. If we don't compromise the principles, then we can rest assured that the foundation will stand through every test of time and every traumatic situation. As you think about people right now and look at different types of businesses available, you can take a look at organizations and individuals in the same industry and see how some of them reach a slow demise and you can practically watch them falling apart. Some businesses, because of their foundation, I can assure you, have properly aligned themselves with the God of the universe, and because of the personal and intimate relationship that they have, their businesses will stand.

When the children of Israel were in Egypt dealing with oppression, before the Lord delivered them from bondage, they were in the same environment, the same space. Yet, they had a relationship. They were protected and they cried out unto the Lord, so He covered them in that oppression, even while Pharaoh was being plagued. Because your relationship is intact and you have a proper prayer life, you respond and listen to the Word of God then act on what He says. No matter what the circumstance, no matter what the world that we exist in may be experiencing, because you call on the name of the Lord and He is your foundation and the very purpose you do everything, you can always expect Him to act on your behalf and defend your place of business. Because you've allowed the presence and the space of God to dwell in your workplace and you watch the way you carry yourself, people will be able to sense there's something different about you. Supernaturally, this will always attract the right long-lasting relationships.

Prayer is key. I challenge each and every one of you to rise up early and plan out your day in prayer and petition the Lord to guide and direct your paths for that particular day. I know in my personal life, on the days when I've been lackluster in getting up and seeking the face of God, I've seen a difference in the way my day goes; things have caught me off guard. When I've taken the time out to spend intimate personal time with Him early in the morning prior to my day getting underway, I've been able to navigate through things. I'm able to see things and experience a different type of day because I'm alert and my awareness is different. Being with Him allows me to function and operate in that supernatural realm of the favor of Lord.

CHAPTER 6

—⟨⟨⟨⟩⟩⟩—

Obedience

""What is more pleasing to the LORD: your burnt offerings and sacrifices or your obedience to his voice? Obedience is far better than sacrifice. Listening to him is much better than offering the fat of rams."

1 Samuel 15:22

*I*n every chapter, we attempt to help you understand the fundamental spiritual practices of building a successful business and life. Each chapter is a piece of the puzzle and we add on piece by piece to correlate what you may experience on a day-to-day basis. More importantly, we expose you to understanding the concept of spiritual laws and practical living in regard to establishing business in the marketplace and also establishing a firm foundation in your personal life. So many times individuals try to separate the two, but you cannot separate them and expect to succeed.

In this dialogue, we are going to talk about the concept of obedience and having the strength and ability to obey. It's something that's not necessarily easy although the concept sounds simple. The ability to obey is not easy. If it were, more people would heed the Word of God and His instructions in the development of their businesses and their personal lives. This whole concept of obedience stems from the underlying lesson in chapter 3, where we explored *the idea of being able to hear, not only with the ears attached to your head, but also with the ear that is in your heart.* Being able to understand the Word of God and the commandments that are available through Scripture is one thing, but the ability to take the action necessary in order to follow instructions is a whole different ball game. We know that Scripture talks about wisdom. *"Knowledge is the principle thing, but in all thy getting, get understanding."* Proverbs 4:7 What you do with that understanding is directly correlated with your ability to heed the voice and Word of God. Throughout Scripture, and specifically in Deuteronomy, chapter 28, the Word of God speaks of blessings and curses. Deuteronomy talks about the laws of God. If we look in Deuteronomy 11:27, it says:

"You will be blessed if you obey the commands of the LORD your God that I am giving you today"

Then, there's a curse in the following verse:

"You will receive a curse if you reject the commands of the LORD your God and turn from his way by worshiping foreign gods." Deuteronomy 11:28

So, it's very clear that the concept of obedience is the key to instruction as it relates to creating the lifestyles that we desire in our business and personal relationships. If we jump to Job 36:11, it says:

"If they listen and obey God, then they will be blessed with prosperity throughout their lives. All their years will be pleasant." Job 36:11

So, yes, it's very clear, this whole concept of obedience and obeying the commands of God are key, as you work to subject your physical and mental desires to the will that God has for you from a spiritual standpoint—allowing that Spirit Word that He has put inside your heart, as well as in the Scriptures, to be the guiding force. From that same spiritual standpoint, it's not going to be a sensual experience as it relates to what you experience in your physical body. There is going to be some satisfaction from the mental standpoint of having a certain body of knowledge and recognizing that, if you take certain steps based on the information you receive, you'll arrive at your desired outcome. Here, you obtain the satisfaction of understanding, having taken those proper actions. The Word of God is placed in us in a way that allows our human form to operate as it was designed to. Our bodies were not designed to succumb to sensual pleasures or mental gymnastics, but were really designed to allow the Spirit that's within us to rule the human system, our triune system of mind, body, and spirit. The guiding force will be that Spirit of God that's within us.

Many times, we disobey in doing the things that we know we should do and end up putting our physical form and mind in distress because we're not working in the way that our system was designed to work. Again, we must recognize that our spirit is in constant enmity with the body. After all, the body is flesh while the spirit within us wants to and should be in sync with God and His Word. Throughout Scripture, it certainly talks about obedience and the reward of obeying the voice of the Lord and what the outcome will be for those who refuse to obey. I know one of the interesting questions in Scripture is found in Exodus where Pharaoh asks why he should heed the voice of Moses and obey the voice of God. This is found in the book of Exodus, where Pharaoh asks:

"Is that so?" retorted Pharaoh. "And who is the LORD that I should listen to him and let Israel go? I don't know the LORD, and I will not let Israel go." Exodus 5:2

Because he had no knowledge of the Lord, Pharaoh was questioning who the Lord was. Pharaoh didn't recognize that he should obey, and though he wasn't of the tribe of Israel, if he had known who the Lord was, he would have heeded the words of Moses when he requested that Pharaoh let His people go. Ignorance is not necessarily an excuse, but having the foreknowledge of God, the commandments, and the Word of God puts you in a position that makes it even more critical for you to obey those things that are spiritual—allow your mind and body to fall in line with the Word of God. We all know the outcome of Pharaoh and his army. His heart was hardened and he made bad decisions as a result of it. He was given every opportunity to recognize who God was through all of the signs and wonders that God performed through Moses and Pharaoh still chose not to obey. He was given more than ten opportunities to heed the words of God uttered by Moses and Aaron.

This is very similar to our own lives, as we work to build businesses and relationships. We pretty much know the things that we need to and should do, and we have the information that tells us how to get from point A to point B. We know how to develop the stamina, how to develop the habits and work ethic—all of that information is there. Sometimes though, we get off of our path because we know we're not really in line with the things that we should be doing. Obedience to spiritual law, to mental law, and to natural law are things that are required for us to be able to operate in an optimal way in order for us to reach the success that we're looking for. As God talks and we obey, we can certainly have *success on God's terms* in the sense that He has set forth the law and the commandments. His requirement is that we obey! It is better to obey on the front end than to have to sacrifice because of disobedience and to give up something in order to get forgiveness from the Lord. The great thing about grace and understanding this whole concept of obedience is that we have the ability, once we are disobedient, to repent and obey and we can still fall in line with the blessings and those things that God has set up for us, as we work to follow His lead and instruction and guidance.

So, obedience is certainly key and it does take strength to obey. Obedience might not seem as much fun or pleasurable as other things but, in the long run, we have the opportunity to reap the rewards from a prosperity standpoint. We're not just talking about money, but about the peace and joy that resides within those who follow the leading example of God through Christ Jesus. Obedience is a key element, so it's not enough to know or understand. With that knowledge and understanding, you have to take the appropriate action (and make sure it lines up with God) and you must follow the instruction, or the system, or follow those who have walked the path by example and have been given an opportunity to illustrate what it is to obey and reap the blessings. This dialogue is very basic and clear. Disobedience comes with a price and penalty. Sometimes, that price is the death of your soul or physical body because you have not followed the laws that have been decreed by God. Sometimes, that price is the death of your business or a relationship with someone, if you are walking outside the law or the command that God has laid out for you. Because of His grace and mercy, He allows us to fall down, pick ourselves up, repent, and continue to walk in obedience and build up our spiritual muscles in regard to having the strength to obey and stand in the midst of all that comes against us. Then we can be obedient when faced with unscrupulous sensual pleasures or wicked mental gymnastics that we go through sometimes. Being popular or smart do get you noticed, but those are not our first priorities and we can't just be hearers of the Word; we must be doers of the Word. In recognizing that, the whole concept of being doers of the Word takes us back to the original concept of obedience.

Once again, it is extremely important that we understand how obedience leads to every positive action and, of course, when we negate obedience, there's the opposite of that, which is disobedience. Scripture is very clear in regard to whether or not we are obedient and how it allows us to experience wealth. Everything is always going to be tied into our willingness to obey or disobey. When we look at the word *obey* in its simplest form, it means "to conform or give in; to execute; support." It also has to do with good behavior because, out of obedience, God's law is irrefutable. If we are willing to obey, there are some wonderful things we can acquire or obtain simply by being obedient.

I want to share with you the word from Isaiah 1:19 on the importance of following the Word of God. There's one particular verse of Scripture that says, *"If ye be willing and obedient, ye shall eat the good of the land"*. That's coming from the King James Version, but I also want to read into your hearing from the New Living Translation to give you a present-day reality of what this means:

> *"If you will only obey me and let me help you, then you will have plenty to eat. But if you keep turning away and refusing to listen, you will be destroyed by your enemies. I, the LORD, have spoken!"* Isaiah 1:19–20

There's a promise that comes with being obedient, and as we look at the Word of God and the word *obedient*, it actually appears sixteen times in the King James Bible. As the men and women of God obeyed His voice, there was always increase. So, when we look at applying this to our day-to-day living, what happens? If you're willing to obey the laws of the land, then you will produce the fruit that's going to allow you to experience the goodness. As you're looking at your business, as you're looking at your day-to-day operations and how you deal with and dwell with people, sometimes it's very difficult to be obedient because our natural nature is against aligning itself with the ability to follow instruction. Here is the important part: even at the beginning, in the garden, the commandment was given and God told Adam and Eve that they could eat from every tree, except one in particular. Then, out of their eventual disobedience, humankind was propelled into a sinful nature, which literally disrupted the initial game plan God intended for you and me from the very beginning.

So, it's significant that you understand that with our natural nature comes the inclination to supersede our spiritual nature; this happens because we've not fed our soul by consuming the Word of God. Remember the battle that's constantly raging between the body (which is the flesh) and our spirit rages in our mind, emotions and intellect (our soul). As we find ourselves consuming the Word of God, it gives us the ability to walk out our spiritual awareness and have it manifested in the natural by being obedient.

This is really simple in the sense that, if you obey the Word of God, there are promises tied into your obedience—it's just not easy to do. If you choose not to follow the Word of God and give in to that physical nature, there are consequences tied into your disobedience. The crux of the matter is, it's better to be obedient than to sacrifice or go through the ritualistic aspect of pretending because, even when we think we're doing or sacrificing, we have to recognize that obedience is that which is going to please God *first*. Because our devotion and ability to please God is first and primary in our lives, we can trust, we can believe, and we can have hope in the fact that God will do what He says He will do. He basically says, *"If you seek Me first and do what I ask you to do and do what I purpose you to do, then you will be able to receive all the entitlements of my heirs because you have followed my instructions."*

That's the main point of obedience and that's how important it is, even in the day-to-day operation and function of your business. There are laws and guidelines that we must adhere to, and if we adhere to those, then we can expect, we can trust, and we can know that our businesses will reap the returns and the investment will be made manifest. So, if you're looking right now at your current situation, my challenge to you is to ask yourself how obedient have you been.

Everything that we're talking about, from a manifestation in the natural for your businesses, is tied into your being obedient to the Word of God. This means that our responsibility is to be obedient to the Word of God first and, by doing that, we will experience the benefit, in due season—the prosperity that's tied into living according to the Word of God. I just want to add this verse of Scripture for you from Psalm 1 KJV:

"Blessed is the man that walketh not in the counsel of the ungodly, nor standeth in the way of sinners, nor sitteth in the seat of the scornful. But his delight is in the law of the Lord; an in his law doth he mediate day and night" Psalm 1:1-2 KJV

The obedient believer obeys the Word of God and meditates on it day and night.

"And he shall be like the tree planted by the rivers of water, that bringeth forth his fruit in his season; and his leaf shall not wither; and whatsoever he doeth shall prosper." Psalm 1:3 KJV

These things are tied into obedience and living out what the Word of God says. Here's the contrast to not being obedient to the Word of God. It says:

"The ungodly are not so: but are like the chaff which the wind driveth away. Therefore the ungodly shall not stand in the judgment, nor sinners in the congregation of the righteous. For the LORD knoweth the way of the righteous: but the way of the ungodly shall perish." Psalm 1:4-6 KJV

So, we have the option to obey, but out of obedience, we can expect, we can anticipate, we can receive, and we can believe the manifestation of the promises of God.

On that note, I want to share with you and highlight the importance of, your being obedient and walking out your plans in the natural, on a spiritual basis. Because we allow our spiritual nature to supersede our natural, we can anticipate the supernatural taking over our personal lives as well as our business endeavors, knowing that God is a God of multiplication and replication and we've been given a commandment to take dominion, to subdue, and to replenish. Out of our obedience, we can expect our natural lives to be enhanced because of His supernatural power, which will ultimately bring glory and honor to the God of the universe.

Just one closing thought before we explore the concept of *humility*. In Philippians 2, there's a description of the obedience of Christ as an example. It starts in verse 5,

"Let this mind be in you, which is also in Christ, who being in the form of God thought it not robbery to be equal with God, but made himself of no reputation and took upon him the form of a servant, and was made in the likeness of men; And being found in fashion as a man, he humbled himself and became obedient unto death, even the death of the cross. Wherefore, God hath also highly exalted him, and given him a name which is above every name: That at the name of Jesus, every knee should bow, of things in heaven and things in earth and things under the earth; And that every tongue should confess that Jesus Christ is Lord, to the glory of God the Father." Philippians 2:5–11

So, even Christ was obedient to the will of His Father God, our Father in Heaven. Jesus paid the ultimate price and was obedient to the cost that He had to pay. His name is above every name, not only in Heaven, but on and under the earth. This means all places that exist are subject to the Lordship of Christ Jesus. It was because of His humility and obedience, even unto death, that we have the chance to get it right in our own lives. Our obedience needs to be, not *so* drastic as being nailed to a cross and taking on the sins of past, present, and future generations, but we certainly need to become obedient to the extent that we have an opportunity to kill our own personal desires, and to do so for the greater good—so that we can replace evil thoughts with the thoughts of God. These are a few of the things that fall under the concept of obedience and following the Word of God the Father.

CHAPTER 7

—⁓⁓—

Humility

"Then if my people who are called by my name will humble themselves and pray and seek my face and turn from their wicked ways, I will hear from heaven and will forgive their sins and heal their land."

2 Chronicles 7:14

C. Thomas Gambrell's Testimony

This subject of humility was one that I had to learn, I would say, the hard way in the sense that it was not really part of my character as I was growing into my adolescence and young adulthood. It was a lesson that I had to learn in my walk with Jesus as I turned my life over to Him in a sacrificial way. I wasn't really able to understand what He was about until I was able to humble myself. At a very young age, I excelled in baseball to the point where, at the age of 12, I was being recruited by high school coaches. They were talking to my grandmother, at the time, when I was living with her in Tampa, Florida, about moving me to my aunt's address or at least putting her address on my high school application to make sure I was in the right school district to attend their particular high school. With success in sports sometimes comes a big ego. When I started building network marketing businesses in the mid nineties, I stood five feet seven, but I would often tell people that I used to be six feet two because my head was so big. I had a *really* big ego! Having the opportunity to excel at sports and to attend an Ivy League institution occurred not just because of my athletic ability,

I also had the grades and test scores to be accepted to Columbia University. Being a graduate of that university and working on Wall Street at a very young age while earning a six-figure income put me in a position where I was actually making more money at that time than my parents and my spouse combined. So, as an African American male at the age of twenty-seven doing things my parents dreamed I would, I was really in a situation where that came with a lot of ego. God has a way of showing you yourself and helping you understand that, although you might be having success on certain levels with material gain or you've been able to excel from an athletic standpoint, in His eyes, He's not measuring that; He judges the content of your heart. He had to really show me myself. That mirror being placed in my face allowed me to recognize that I didn't have it all together, that a lot of it was really a front because, although I was making a six figure income, I also had six figure debt between student loans, credit cards, bad investments, and horrible spending habits. Although I was doing things my parents dreamed I would do, I'd never sacrificed to put a child through elementary or high school or paid for an education. I certainly couldn't pay for anything myself at the time when I was going through school. The measurement of who we are and where we are a lot of times comes through our eyes and our experiences. We have to recognize that God speaks to us and we must listen for what He would have us do. That brings me to the foundation Scripture for this chapter. It comes from 2 Chronicles 7:14 and it reads:

> *"If My people who are called by My name shall humble themselves, and pray and seek My face, and turn away from their wicked ways, then I will hear from heaven, and will forgive their sin and will heal their land."*

This is quite a significant Scripture for me in the sense that the first thing He says in this instruction is in regard to the course of action that we are to take in order to open the gates of heaven to receive the blessings that He has dictated for us. It simply says, *"If My people who are called by My name shall humble themselves. .".* I find it very interesting that the humility piece came first. The instruction could have been "seek My face" first or "turn from your wicked ways" first or "to pray," but *humility* really opens up the gates. Sometimes people think that humility is a weak position, but really the concept of humility or being humble is something that gives you all the power that's available to you from the Creator. He's saying that if you humble yourselves and then take these actions—praying, seeking His face, and turning from your wicked ways—He will hear you and He will forgive you and then He will heal you. I think that's a very positive formula to understand, how to open yourself up to receive the blessings of God.

We know that Jesus, just taking on the form of a man, coming in the flesh as a man, certainly humbled Himself with regard to the affinity that He shares with God the Father as well as the Holy Spirit. So, that was the ultimate humility, infinity finding itself encapsulated in human flesh and taking on all of the emotions as well as the frailties of the human disposition. We know that is ultimate humility because all power exists with Christ Jesus and all things in Heaven and earth bow before Him. He made Himself a servant and came to show us the way in the form of human flesh.

As you're looking at your business, when you're engaging in day-to-day action for the company that you represent, who are you really willing to honor and serve? Based on those opportunities, that humility will supersede your agenda, but more importantly, it will promote the agenda in which you've been inspired and which you've been called to. As we look at the dynamics of humility, from a servant's standpoint, Jesus set the example. He said,

> *"But among you, those who are the greatest should take the lowest rank, and the leader should be like a servant. Normally the master sits at the table and is served by his servants. But not here! For I am your servant."* Luke 22:26–27

So as we look at servanthood, that is the key ingredient that will allow your business to grow. The beautiful thing about having the spirit of humility, as it's written in Proverbs 18:16, the Word of God declares that ". . .*your gift will make room for you and bring you before great men.*" The gift that you have will never be realized or manifest itself until you've humbled yourself. As we think about ego, the word can be viewed as an acronym. The word *ego* could stand for "edging God out," so anytime we act as if we don't need the God of the universe to act on our behalf, understand that to be a mistake. The Scripture explains His desire for each of us as shared in 2 Chronicles 7:14 above. If you read the previous verses, the famine and the feast were sent by God to help the children of Israel realize that, if He didn't act or intervene on their behalf, all of those calamities would take over and it would be detrimental. So, as you're functioning and operating in your business, you must come to the realization that God is the head of your business. If you don't, you cannot expect your business to flourish, not until you humble yourself and seek the will of God and have Him infused into everything you do.

Because of your humility, there is a promise that, whatever you put your hand to, because it's purposed and you've turned it over to Him, He will dwell in it. God is a God of multiplication and that privilege now becomes a part of your inheritance once you realize that you can do nothing absent of Him intervening on your behalf.

As I was doing the commentary on 2 Chronicles 7:14, it seemed to be a very simple process, talking about the equation and concept of humility. Yet, looking back, I remember, as I was going through those mental gymnastics as a young man, I really thought *I* was the source and the cause of all these phenomenal things happening to me and for me. We spoke in the introduction about the faith of our mothers. I was really riding on the prayers of my grandparents and my parents and not really going on much steam from myself. You can only thrive on the prayers offered by someone else for so long before you have to begin to do for yourself—praying and seeking

God's face and turning from the sin that's prevalent in all of our lives.

As we humble ourselves, God will hear us as we begin to turn from the life that is without Him and turn to Him as our source. He will forgive every sin. As we repent and turn to Him, we also have the promise of healing. It's not just the land itself being healed, but also about each of us being healed.

Living Earth

We, on a fundamental level, are living earth. Every element in our bodies comes from the earth and shall return to the earth. So, there's not only healing for the land, for the community, for the nation, for the people, but also healing for our individual selves, healing from those things that plague us and the things that we try to cover up and hide—things that God certainly knows about. We turn those things over to Him through our humility and understand that He's the One; He's the Source; He's the One who is going to assist us as we deal with life by humbling ourselves in His presence, before the majesty of the Creator. He will heal us mentally, emotionally, and physically. Then, when we align all those things with the Word of God, we will also affect our finances. He has made these promises to us if we follow His lead and His Word. He's the Creator of it all. We have an opportunity to follow the equation that's found throughout Scripture, and 2 Chronicles 7:14 is one of the most powerful. Let's look at it again:

> "If My people which are called by My name will humble themselves, and pray and seek My face, and turn from their ways, then I will her from heaven, and will forgive their sin and heal their land."

There are a couple of other verses of Scripture that you can use for references. We have Proverbs 29:23 KJV,

"A man's pride shall bring him low, but honour shall uphold the humble in spirit."

Proverbs 16:19 KJV,

"Better is it to be of a humble spirit with the lowly, than divide the spoils with the proud."

Proverbs 6:3,

"Do this now, my son, and deliver thyself, when thou art come into the hand of thy friend; go, humble thyself, and make sure thy friend."

So, we have these instructions throughout Scripture. Psalm 10:17 also states,

"LORD, Thou hast heard the desire of the humble: Thou wilt prepare their heart, Thou wilt cause thine ear to hear."

It should certainly give you some insight into the significance of the word *humility*, especially the stories that surround the whole concept of humility in the Old Testament.

In Job 22:29 KJV, it says,

"When men are cast down, Then thou shalt say, There is lifting up; and he shall save the humble person."

Even in the story of Job, humility was part of the process that God purposed in him while allowing him to go through his trials.

Because of your humility, you will interact with the right types of individuals. The Word of God says in 2 Corinthians 13:5 that we *"should examine ourselves."* So, where are you? Would those in your center of influence consider you to be an humble person? Are you compelling people or are you repelling people? If you're compelling people, then stay in that vein and continue to walk in a spirit of humility. As in the dialogue, because of our prideful hearts, walking and lacking humility, our businesses will never flourish the way they were intended to and, if you are having success, it will be temporary because the Lord of the universe loves you so much that He does not desire for you to be consumed by anything that's going to replace or separate you from Him. According to the Word of God in Matthew 6:33:

"Seek the Kingdom of God above all else, and live righteously, and he will give you everything you need."

So, there's privilege, there's honor, there's a purpose, and there's a gift. Submit yourself to the Kingdom of God, and because you do that, then you'll be allowed to participate in all the fruits that represent His presence in your life. I just want to end there and say to those of you who have not come into a true understanding of your responsibility, there is a remedy for what seems to be a lack of success. It all starts with knowing you've been separated from the God of the universe, if you have not acknowledged the death, burial, and resurrection of Jesus Christ. By acknowledging this truth and accepting the fact that you've been purposely separated because of your sinful nature, the blood of Jesus Christ has the power to remove that gulf. By doing that and receiving this gift, you have the opportunity to walk and be re-born spiritually into the family of God—to partake in all the wonderful things available to you as an heir.

So, how do you have success? First of all, are you submitting yourself and do you realize that without this relationship you cannot function properly? We know we are in right relationship with Him when we think like Him and we speak the Word that He's given us, the Word of God. Then, we take the necessary actions and we perform, allowing the Spirit of God to operate and work through us. After doing that, you'll receive the manifestation of the Kingdom of Heaven on earth. This is the remedy and how you have *success on God's terms*, and now that we've done it the way God instructed us to do it, we can expect Him to heal our land. We can expect Him to defend and fight on our behalf. More importantly, we can expect Him to prosper us because we now realize it's not because of our gifts or strength, but by His Spirit and His might and all glory and honor will go to Him. Now, because you understand this, you can expect to make an impact, not only in your local community, but in the world.

PART 2

The Creation Equation

CHAPTER 8

⟨∂/∂⟩

THINK Segment

"But let us who live in the light think clearly, protected by the body armor of faith and love, and wearing as our helmet the confidence of our salvation."

1 Thessalonians 5:8

*I*t is impossible to do anything that you haven't first thought about. It sounds like a simple concept, right? As we talk about this philosophy of *success on God's terms*, the concept of *thinking* is a key element in the equation of creation. Are you thinking the thoughts that you have come up with on your own or are you basing your thoughts on the Word of God? What does the Word of God say about the different aspects of your life? Thinking is a key factor in your success, and not just thinking, but accurate thinking rooted in the unchanging Word of the Creator of the universe.

Philosophers, through the ages, have said that most people don't think. This is the case because others often do the thinking for them most of their lives. From birth, we are told what to do by others. Stop crying, go to sleep, be quiet, time to eat. No! Don't! Stop! Children are always being instructed what to do, when to do it, and how to go about it. We grill them on the importance of going to school, then on to college or the military and, eventually into the job market. You have an opportunity to break out of that cycle as you take ownership of your person and your life.

I think of the Book of Genesis often and about how important chapter one is as it relates to the phrase *"God said."* Even though God had already thought about what He wanted to do as it related to creating man in His image, He still spoke it. He spoke and that created a force, which manifested itself in the physical realm. You have to speak those things that are not as though they were, in order to call them into existence. If the proper thoughts are not there, then what you speak will only be a shadow of what you intended to create. You end up creating something that is not going to benefit you. Your thoughts have to be grounded in something that is infallible and something that is unshakable, which is the Word of God.

Much like a play, the script for your success in life has already been written. God knows the outcome of the play and the victory that awaits us as it relates to eternal life, but we still have to perform here in the natural—in time and space. We have a choice to make. The choice that God has given us through the gift of free will is whether we will follow His script or do our own thing. Regardless of what we decide, we still have to perform to get the intended outcome of His script or the one we write. We still have to think those thoughts and speak those words. Then, we have to take the appropriate action to bring what we've spoken into existence. We know that, although plays have been written and the scripts are in place, the actors sometimes get on stage and forget a line or they say the wrong words or move to the wrong part of the stage. So, even though it's been written, we still have to perform. In that final piece, in anticipation of what that performance is, not only will we have an opportunity to see, but the entire world will have an opportunity to see those things that we've been able to create.

The idea is that we are citizens of Heaven and earth and, as we are here to occupy, we have to make sure that the Kingdom of Heaven is manifested here on earth through our thoughts and our speech, as well as our performance. As those things line up, there's nothing that you won't be able to create, including those good things that are waiting for you.

Think Segment

This is the equation for creation and creating *success on God's terms*. The process of thinking proper thoughts is going to be key to your success because your language and actions are framed by your thoughts. You cannot think or speak beyond information and knowledge that you have been exposed to in your life. So, those things that we dwell on in our minds are the things that we talk about and the things that we end up taking action on. Then, we begin to see the results in the earthly realm of the things that we meditate on daily.

The Scriptural reference for this dialogue is from the Book of Joshua 1:8–9. In the King James Bible, it reads:

"This book of the law shall not depart out of thy mouth; but thou shalt meditate therein day and night, that thou mayest observe to do according to all that is written therein: for then thou shalt make thy way prosperous, and then thou shalt have good success. Have not I commanded thee? Be strong and of a good courage ; be not afraid, neither be thou dismayed : for the LORD thy God is with thee whithersoever thou goest"
Joshua 1:8–9 KJV

The whole concept of meditating on the Word gives you an opportunity to transfer the information in Scripture from the book into your mind. You don't just want to read the words, but to meditate *on* the words and make them part of your thought process. Make them part of your thinking, which will allow the transfer to take place from the Word of God into your mind as part of the things that you focus on daily, moment by moment. The opportunity that you have is in understanding what this simple instruction says, to meditate day and night, and to apply it.

Meditation is something that is more than just reading or taking in information. It's really about pondering the information; it's about thinking hard about what's being said to you in different parts of Scripture and how it applies to your life today, how it applies to your business, how it applies to your ability to make the Word of God relevant to your business and to your life and your daily activities. We also use this concept of thinking as part of our coaching practice, where we talk to our clients about what they are doing with their time.

Concept of Time

What you're doing with your time really dictates what you do with your life. The concept of time management is related to your thinking, in the sense that what you are planning for your life today are the things that you need to focus on doing tomorrow. You should have planned for today as it relates to moving your agenda forward from a business standpoint as well as from a personal standpoint. There are things that need to happen in order for you to achieve the goals that you have set for yourself. Now, whether you have planned these things out in advance or wake up in the morning and determine exactly what you're going to do in the coming day is really based on what you're thinking about and what your thoughts are grounded in.

Thinking is a key component for any kind of success that you would like to have. If you're talking about *success on God's terms*, we have the best reference, the Word of God, to help us figure out what our thinking should be centered on, which is the ability to create success. Scripture is definitely the foundation for good success or what I'd like to call God's success. We have clear instructions in the book, in the Word that God has given to us through the Bible. These are instructions for living and these instructions, when we really take heart and take hold of them, give us the opportunity to have this success outlined in our lives.

Deuteronomy: The Blessings and the Curses

When I first read the Book of Deuteronomy, it had a profound impact on me. That first time I read it, I was an adult in my early thirties and considered myself a Christian. I've considered myself saved since 1991, but it wasn't until 1998 that I actually read the law that was given in the Book of Deuteronomy. It contains both blessings and curses, in the sense that, in God's Word, He dictates conditional and unconditional covenants followed up with instructions given in the law. We have a choice to make as to whether we want the blessings to chase us down or the curses. In chapters 27 and 28, the Word speaks of those things that will overtake you by following the Word of God and those things that will overtake you for *not* following the Word. I want you to go and read the text for yourself and send either of us a message on Facebook to give feedback on your experience in reading the chapters. Just leave your comment on http://www.facebook.com/successongodsterms.

Even though I wasn't aware of it when I first read the text, I saw the curses that were being applied to my life because of the sin that was apparent in some of the actions I was taking or *not* taking according to the Word of God. At the same time, I saw some of the blessings that I was receiving based on following part of those things that were written in the law without even being conscious of them. The concept of thinking and meditating on the Word of God daily, once you know how to do it properly, creates in you a responsibility and accountability to follow those things that are going to lead you to the type of success that God talks about throughout Scripture, in the Old Testament as well as the New Testament.

Philippians 4:8

As we look at this, it gives us the leeway and the understanding that we actually have the ability to control our thought processes. That's why Romans 12:2 conveys *"daily we've got to be renewed and we are to be stricken by the renewing of our mind."* If we put the right information in our mind, it will eliminate a lot of the impure, improper thoughts that we have. It is a matter of continuously saturating our natural database with the proper mindset. This is paramount for you in understanding that you are not to get trapped where you are right now based on your past efforts and your past deficiencies, but continually move forward, thinking on those things that are good. We are reminded of this in the eighth verse of the fourth chapter of Philippians, which reads:

> "And now, dear brothers and sisters, let me say one more thing as I close this letter. Fix your thoughts on what is true and honorable and right. Think about things that are pure and lovely and admirable. Think about things that are excellent and worthy of praise." Philippians 4:8

So, these are the things that are going to allow you to prosper versus your working toward having negative outcomes. As you put positive thoughts in your mind, you have an opportunity to meditate on those things, the things you will speak as you think about them. These are the things that your actions will be focused on because these are the things that your thoughts are founded and grounded in. If you're not thinking about positive things, you certainly can't take positive actions.

I'm talking about actions that you dictate and not about you reacting to something that is happening on the outside of you. I'm talking about you taking action due to those things that are coming from within your heart. As you think and ponder on the good things in life, those are the things that you'll be focused on. If you ponder and think about the negative or bad outcomes stemming from fear or the things that you *don't* want in your life, and if all you think about is what you don't want your business to be like, what you don't want your family members to do, then because you're focusing on those things those are the things that you're going to be releasing into your life—because that's where your focus is. On the other hand, you can focus on the positive outcomes, actions, and words, and I'm not just talking about thinking happy thoughts, but about pondering those things that are going to lead you toward the outcomes that you desire. This means you're not focusing on your problems; you're focusing on the solutions to any problems or challenges you may have with regard to the development of your business.

Whether it's in your household, your business, your place of employment, or in your educational processes, you need to keep the main thing as the main thing and focus on a positive outcome. If you're continuously looking for solutions, you're going to find those solutions that you're looking for. If we're focusing on the things that God has laid out for us in His Word and stored up for us as believers in His Son Jesus, we will be rewarded—even non-believers get rewards as they unconsciously use some of the principles that are found in Scripture.

The natural law is what it is and the spiritual law is what it is. The spiritual blessings, as well as the curses, have been laid out. This isn't the same as having a hex put on you. If you go to the roof of a twelve-story building and you step off the edge, you will certainly fall to the ground. That's a physical law in operation, the law of gravity. If I tell you that, whether you believe it or not, if you take action and step off the edge, you're going to experience the outcome I described to you. Your belief in the law of gravity is irrelevant. The law is going to operate in your life the way it's supposed to, whether you're conscious of it or not. The Scripture is there as a blueprint for us and describes exactly what the outcomes are for various actions that we take. As we grow in our understanding of the things of God and increase in our knowledge and relationship with God, it gives us the ability to strengthen that relationship and create a knowledge transfer that takes place as we read more and more Scripture.

Just like when you're getting to know someone, whether a friend or someone you're in an intimate relationship with, the more time you spend with the person, the more you learn about them. The more you learn about them, the more you see things that you like and some things that you may not like so much, but your knowledge is increased based on how you interact with that person. So, if we take the opportunity to meditate on the Word of God, we'll certainly get to know more about God and the outcomes dictated by certain actions we take. This relates directly to the development of your business as you meditate on the plans you have and the processes you've put in place to create the opportunity to eventually move into a positive outcome.

The timeframe is different for everyone. The same applies to your intimate relationships and your relationships with co-workers, supervisors, and people who report to you. Whatever situation you find yourself in and wherever your thoughts are focused will dictate what is going to happen in your life.

Forty Thousand Thoughts

It is said that on a daily basis we have about fifty to sixty thousand thoughts in a twenty-four hour timeframe. Our minds are constantly working. Even when we're asleep, our minds are working on issues and challenges. Some of that is reflected in the dreams that we have, based on what we were thinking about right before we went to sleep. There could have been a challenge that we had during the day or, in some instances, if you're in the habit of falling asleep with the TV on, which is a very bad habit, your subconscious mind picks up that information while you're asleep. We've all had the experience of falling asleep with the TV on and we wind up dreaming about the movie that's playing in the background of our mind or about whatever show is on the television. So, your mind is constantly at work. The thing about having those fifty to sixty thousand thoughts running through our minds every day is that forty thousand of them are the same thoughts that we had the previous day. This means that, from day-to-day, we are thinking about and pondering the same things most of the time. It's just a matter of what those forty thousand thoughts are that you carry from day-to-day. The forty thousand thoughts that you had yesterday and you're going to have today and tomorrow—are those things that are going to work toward your good and your success in the different facets of your life. Or are you carrying thoughts of negativity, defeat, and failure from day-to-day? Are you focusing on things that are going to lead you toward your destination? Whether it's concerning what you put in your body, what you're putting in your mind, how you're treating people, or how you plan to treat people, when it comes to the schemes you are coming up with in your thoughts, are these things going to lead you toward the good things in life or are they things that are going to lead you to the bad and the negative things in life?

When you're talking about creating success, if you're talking about establishing your kingdom here on earth, pertaining to your ability to have commerce, you need to have property that's going to allow your family to have stability. Do you have the ability to secure your future, concerning what's happening with your children, with your parents, your grandparents—or what's happening with your nuclear family as well as your extended family? How much control do you have over those things? Are you thinking about estate planning? Are you thinking about the next generation and how you're going to set them up for the next twenty to one hundred years? What are the things that you're contemplating on a daily basis? What actions are you taking to make those things come to fruition? What results are you seeing? It's said that fruit doesn't fall far from the tree, that "you shall know them by their fruit". So, look at the anticipated outcomes. You show me a set of outcomes and I'll show you what a person has been thinking about on a daily basis. If death and destruction are outcomes, then that's what that person has been pondering, tragic situations. If they produce something self-inflicted based on actions, interactions, or irresponsibility, you can see that things don't happen for that person a lot of the time; they're steeped in stagnation. There is some level of premeditation and forethought going into the good things of life, as well as in those outcomes that are not deemed so positive.

You have to think about this process of creating your success. You have the opportunity to set the foundation for the success that you're looking for. There are plenty of other references in Scripture that speak to curses and blessings and those you can glean for yourself, but a starting point is Joshua 1:8, Philippians 4:8, as well as the law that is described throughout the Book of Deuteronomy, especially in chapters 27 and 28.

Chapter 9

———❦———

SPEAK Segment

"Now go, and do as I have told you. I will help you speak well, and I will tell you what to say."

Exodus 4:12

*T*his segment is about the next element in the creation equation: speaking. It illustrates the power of the creative vibration in your voice. This, too, is a very simple message: your voice has creative power and you can have what you say. Most of the time, we do have what we say. We're not talking about belief, but what actually comes out of your mouth. We have a tendency to sometimes counteract any positive belief that we have with the negative things that we speak. You have to be in a position where you can recognize the creative force in your voice. You might believe one thing that's very positive, but if you're talking about it using negative terminology all the time, which is the opposite of the belief you're trying to convey, more than likely you're manifesting the negative thing, which is the opposite of what your beliefs might be internally.

If you are actually speaking into the air, you could very well speak that thing that is the opposite of what you really want, desire, or believe. From a creative standpoint, as you're working to build your business and your family while striving to have an impact in your workplace and to contribute in your place of fellowship, you have to make sure that your thoughts and your speech are congruent. There is going to be a direct link to the type of actions that you take and dictate, leading to the results that you see. So, what you say is a reflection of your thought processes as well as your belief system.

God Said

If we look at the Book of Genesis, we recognize that in the first five verses, it says,

> *"In the beginning God created the heavens and the earth. Now the earth was formless and empty, darkness was over the surface of the deep and the Spirit of God was hovering over the waters. And God said 'Let there be light,' and there was light. God saw the light was good and he separated the light from the darkness. God called the light day and the darkness he called night. And there was evening and there was morning. That was the first day."* Genesis 1:1–5 NIV

We know that God has creative power, but there's something significant about the fact that He said, *"let there be light,"* because certainly, I am of the belief that He could have just thought it and it would have happened. I think this speaking action of God was an illustration for us, set as a pattern of exactly what we need to do in order to manifest something from that which is formless and empty. Speaking gives us the ability to bring light to a situation by understanding what is coming out of our mouths. We know the Scripture talks about life and death being in the power of the tongue and we have the ability, the creative force to build or destroy as we are speaking over situations concerning our businesses, our spouses, our children, and even our elders. We can change situations just by blessing someone with our words. There's a vibration that we put into the universe or into the air that gives us creative power as it relates to having a direct link to the things that we have an opportunity to see.

In criminal justice, we know of the countless testimonies of men and women who are in prison and, if you ask them what their childhood was like and what was being said to them, the answer always seems to be, *"You'll never be anything because you're no good. You're worthless."* These are the types of things these individuals have heard most of their lives and they end up living up to the words that were put into their ears and found there way into their hearts. These ugly words seep into their hearts and embed themselves into their minds, until they finally begin to act out those things and wind up making them decrees and self-fulfilling prophecies. Certainly, they could have chosen to go another route and the people talking to them could have put some positive words in their ears, in their minds, and in their hearts so that outcome would have been positive when it came to fruition.

It doesn't matter what deficiencies you may have from a speaking standpoint. There are things and tools in place that give you the ability to overcome those deficiencies, because of the creative force that rests and abides in you—to literally change your entire perception of who you are and not only your own perception, but it can change the entire atmosphere in which you exist. It's as simple as the beginning of Genesis, where there was darkness and there was chaos. Even right now, your life may be totally chaotic. You may not be in a place where you want to be, but by speaking and saying the proper things in your situation, you will have the ability to see very different things come to fruition, based on what you're saying.

It doesn't matter where you are or if you don't believe, but if you say the right things continually, then that will help shape your reality. In the Bible, the words *the Lord said* appear 835 times; the words *God spoke* appear 53 times in Scripture; and the word *spoken* appears 57 times. The word *speak,* itself appears 94 times; the word *spake,* which is the past tense of *speak,* appears 66 times; the word *saying* appears 396 times in Scripture; and the word *sayeth,* appears

387 times. The word *said*, which is past tense for *say*, appears 615 times; the word *called* appears 603 times; and the present tense of that word, which is *call*, appears 824 times. The word *ask* appears 235 times; the past tense of that, *asked*, appears 113 times. The word *tongue*, meaning the tongue itself, appears 160 times. The word *cry* appears 204 times and the word *voice* appears 409 times. This might help you understand that, where you are presently, is because of the things you've uttered on a continual basis. Here's what happens: We cannot—our *minds* cannot—distinguish between what's real and what is not real. So, whatever you have said to yourself, whatever people have said to you, you've either lived up to it or lived down to that person's perception or expectation of who you are. It's very important for you not only to think properly, but it is also very important for you to repel those things that are contrary to what God has already said you are. As we speak to our mountains, if we would just have the faith of a mustard seed, we could say to that mountain, *"Be thou removed,"* and it would be removed just by speaking it. Whatever the obstacle is, whatever the challenge you may be facing right now, what you say will compel or move those things into action.

Examples of Asking and Receiving

There was a point in time when Joshua needed to have more faith. He was fighting a battle and petitioned the Lord, asking Him to let the sun stand still for a whole day. Upon his request, upon his crying out, the Lord granted that request. Also Elisha the prophet decreed, established, and commanded that it not rain for three years and just at his word, it did *not* rain for three years. When he petitioned the Lord again and spoke, he asked that it rain and instantly the rain began to fall! So, what does that mean? To bring it into the present day and make it personal so that we can apply it right now, I want to let you know that we have the same ability concerning our businesses and our lives. We can speak into and over our businesses, and not only our businesses—we have the ability to speak over our family situations.

We don't just have the ability to speak over them, but to speak over our income and other monies because, in Job 22:28, it said that, *"We shall decree a thing and it shall be established."*

Here's the thing you have to understand as you are reading this information: You have creative force. You have creative power in your voice. My question to each and every one of you right now is: what have you been saying to yourself over the last twenty-four hours? What have you said to yourself over the last two hours? What have you said about your business? What have you said about your ability to move people to action? What is your perception of *you*? What do you speak to yourself on a day-to-day basis? Here's something else I want you to understand: Moses was considered to be one of the greatest deliverers that humanity has ever known. He came to God, but he tried to give God excuses as to why he wasn't the one He needed to send to deliver His people. He told Him,

> *"O Lord, I'm just not a good speaker. I never have been, and I'm not now, even after you have spoken to me. I'm clumsy with words"* Exodus 4:10

He was petitioning the Lord, trying to get out of doing something he'd been predestined to do and the Lord said to him, *"Moses, go and tell Pharaoh to let My people go."* Moses was concerned because he was going to have to return to the very people he had run from, and now he had a mission. So, even now as you're establishing your business, it's important that you're creating the relationships that you need with the people you want to connect to in order to sell the products and/or services that you need to deliver. You are on a mission to succeed. The Lord encouraged Moses, but Moses was concerned about who, when he went to these people, would he say sent him? And the Lord said to Moses, *say"* **I AM** THE ONE WHO ALWAYS IS. Just tell them, '**I AM** has sent me to you". In other words, whatever you need as you speak, whatever you're deficient in, you have the power and ability to walk into that office of authority simply because you've submitted yourself and now you're speaking your total existence into fruition. So, this day, as you examine your business, right where you are, you can operate a profitable enterprise.

Here's the thing, we don't want to put any limits on you, so it does not matter that it has not come to fruition *yet*. It begins with your thought processes first. You have to see it on the inside before you see it on the outside, and as you see it internally, say it. With your saying it, it will come to fruition because, as we stated above, all *was* in total darkness. There was chaos and God said, *"Let there be light,"* and there was light, obliterating the darkness and bringing order. I'm saying to you, with your business, with the relationships you need to establish, and with the integrity that you need to walk in, as you see yourself, see yourself walking in integrity. Then, you can make a proclamation or decree, and if you decree a thing, it shall be established.

Remember, the verse of Scripture to place in your heart and continually mediate on is Job 22:28 KJV, *"Thou shalt decree a thing and it shall be established..."* If you command it, because of the power and the creative force in your voice, it shall be established. The words that you establish, because they are purposed to do the will of God the Father and establish His Kingdom on the earth, will not return to you void. Also, according to Isaiah 55:11, the Word of God will accomplish the purpose for which it was spoken and will not return to Him void or to you void, based on how you utilize the information that we're sharing.

This concept of creative power in spoken words is prevalent throughout Scripture and, in some instances, it is caused just by the vibration coming from your mouth. We look at Joshua 6:3–5, ending with Joshua 6:20. The text outlines the instructions that were given to Joshua as the Israelites were going to Jericho to do battle. We know that Jericho had a fortress and that a wall was protecting the city. Even with the unconventional instructions that God had given Joshua, based on them following the Word of God, they had an opportunity, in verse 20, to actually see that word come to fruition because they followed the instructions that were given as God spoke them to Joshua. It starts in verse 3,

> *"And ye shall compass the city, all ye men of war, and go round about the city once. Thus shalt thou do six days. And seven priests shall bear before the ark seven trumpets of rams' horns; and the seventh day ye shall compass the city seven times, and the priests shall blow with the trumpets. And it shall come to pass, that when they make a long blast with the ram's horn, and when ye hear the sound of the trumpet, all the people shall shout with a great shout; and the wall of the city shall fall down, and the people shall ascend up every man straight before him."* Joshua 6:3–5 KJV

And then, skipping down to verse 20, it basically shows the instructions being followed and the Word of God coming to fruition. So, in verse 20 it says:

> *"So the people shouted when the priests blew the trumpets; and it came to pass, when the people heard the sound of the trumpet, and the people shouted with a great shout, that the wall fell down flat, so that the people went up into the city, every man straight before him, and they took the city."* Joshua 6:20 KJV

This is *all* according to God's Word and they didn't even have to speak a word. They made a great shout with their voices following the instructions of God and certainly got the victory. Just imagine the people that were in the city watching them march around for six days; they marched around once a day for six days not making a sound, but then, BOOM! On the seventh *day*, one blast from their voice knocked the walls down. Not only did they knock the walls down, they knocked them flat. Can you imagine what the effect of all that power was, being released from those voices with those individuals following the Word of God the way they did?

When we look at Scripture, Jesus would, on occasion, bless someone on a word of faith they confessed or showed Him. If we look at the instance of the blind man in Mark 10:51–52, it says:

> *"And Jesus answered and said unto him, What wilt thou that I should do unto thee? The blind man said unto him, Lord, that I might receive my sight. And Jesus said unto him, Go thy way; thy faith hath made thee whole. And immediately he received his sight, and followed Jesus in the way."* Mark 10:51–52 KJV

Now, think about what happened in that instant in the sense that it was obvious to Jesus as He walked up to this man that he was blind. He could have just touched his eyes and his sight would have returned without even an uttered word, but this blind man had to be actively engaged in the process to receive the blessing. Maybe the gentleman was comfortable being blind. Maybe he wanted wealth or a blessing for someone else. God, in the person of Jesus, said, *"Hey, what should I do for you?"* The blind man said unto Him, *"Lord, that I might receive my sight",* and that's what he was blessed with.

Also, when we look in Matthew, chapter 8, there is the story about the Gentile centurion, starting in verse 5, all the way through 13,

> *"When Jesus arrived in Capernaum, a Roman officer came and pleaded with him, "Lord, my young servant lies in bed, paralyzed and racked with pain." Jesus said, "I will come and heal him."Then the officer said, "Lord, I am not worthy to have you come into my home. Just say the word from where you are, and my servant will be healed!"* Matthew 8:5–8

And it goes on,

> *"I know, because I am under the authority of my superior officers and I have authority over my soldiers. I only need to say, 'Go,' and they go, or 'Come,' and they come. And if I say to my slaves, 'Do this or that,' they do it." When Jesus heard this, he was amazed. Turning to the crowd, he said, "I tell you the truth, I haven't seen faith like this in all the land of Israel! And I tell you this, that many Gentiles will come from all over the world and sit down with Abraham, Isaac, and Jacob at the feast in the Kingdom of Heaven. But many Israelites—those for whom the Kingdom was prepared—will be cast into outer darkness, where there will be weeping and gnashing of teeth." Then Jesus said to the Roman officer, "Go on home. What you have believed has happened." And the young servant was healed that same hour."* Matthew 8:9–13

The fact that Jesus didn't have to follow His original plan of going and actually being in the presence of the servant to heal him was based on the word of faith decreed by the centurion who was not even of the Jewish faith. Though he wasn't of the same religion, he had such faith in the ability of God to produce what he needed, he knew just a word from Jesus would be enough to actually heal his loved one. The only way for Christ to share the extent of this centurion's faith was to let him verbally express that faith. As he said, Jesus had but to *"speak the word only and my servant shall be healed."*

So, your voice has creative power, not only for you to follow the instructions of God, but also for you to be a blessing to other people, even when you aren't in the presence of those individuals. When we're praying for people who are facing disasters, like those in New Orleans in 2005, Haiti in 2010, or in Japan in 2011, as we are sending our money and our resources, we need to recognize that the most important thing we need to do in those moments is pray. We need to speak positive words out of our mouths, issuing blessings into the atmosphere. As we witness these situations secondhand by watching the news, we should just start praying right then. When we see a person trapped or a family grieving, we should just start praying and creating healing power. The power in our voice can certainly bless those individuals.

The whole concept, the key thought here is that when you speak, whose words are you using? Are you speaking the opinion of someone else about you in your situation? My understanding or my petition to you is that you should base everything that is happening in your life, in your business and in your family, on the Word of God. His Word will never return void. We know the popular verse from Isaiah 55:11, which reads:

> *"It is the same with my word. I send it out, and it always produces fruit. It will accomplish all I want it to, and it will prosper everywhere I send it."* Isaiah 55:11

If you look at the verses that precede verse 11, as well as the verses that follow verse 11, it gives you the entire context of what He really means when He says, *"I send it out, and it always produces fruit. It will accomplish all I want it to, and it will prosper everywhere I send it..."*

These verses give you a full understanding of the Spirit of the Word. This is Isaiah 55, verses 6 through 13:

> *"Seek the LORD while you can find him. Call on him now while he is near. Let the people turn from their wicked deeds. Let them banish from their minds the very thought of doing*

wrong! Let them turn to the LORD that he may have mercy on them. Yes, turn to our God, for he will abundantly pardon. "My thoughts are completely different from yours," says the LORD. "And my ways are far beyond anything you could imagine. For just as the heavens are higher than the earth, so are my ways higher than your ways and my thoughts higher than your thoughts. "The rain and snow come down from the heavens and stay on the ground to water the earth. They cause the grain to grow, producing seed for the farmer and bread for the hungry. It is the same with my word. I send it out, and it always produces fruit. It will accomplish all I want it to, and it will prosper everywhere I send it. You will live in joy and peace. The mountains and hills will burst into song, and the trees of the field will clap their hands! Where once there were thorns, cypress trees will grow. Where briers grew, myrtles will sprout up. This miracle will bring great honor to the LORD's name; it will be an everlasting sign of his power and love." Isaiah 55:6–13

Just recognize that, as you line up with the thoughts of God and the Word of God, you have an opportunity to have His blessing impact your life in every way. Scripture says *"You will live in joy and peace."* Even nature has to bow down to you as you line up with the Word of God, creating situations and scenarios around you and in other areas of the world that transpire to make your words come to fruition. Right now, as you're talking about your business in a very powerful way, you're talking about generating six or seven figures and things are orchestrating in order for that to happen and come to fruition—things that you are not even aware of. You're just going to walk into it because you've already decreed it and it also aligns with the Word of God. There's nothing that you bring forth that's lined up with the Word of God that shall not be accomplished. It says

> *"Where once there were thorns, cypress trees will grow. Where briers grew, myrtles will sprout up. This miracle will bring great honor to the LORD's name; it will be an everlasting sign of his power and love.*

Then, in the King James Version verse 13 ends with *". . .that shall not be cut off."* That means your purpose shall be established and there's nothing that can come against it, especially when you are using the words of God and taking appropriate actions in order to see positive outcomes.

It takes you being totally honest with yourself, as you digest this information and think about what you've been saying to yourself. Whether you think it or speak it, it's very significant and directly related to where you are right now. As we begin to understand and line up ourselves with the Word of God, the process of seeing what has already been declared, decreed, and established becomes apparent. It is the will of God to prosper you so that you can be reflective and a representative of His authority and His power in the earth.

According to the Word,

> *"A man's belly shall be satisfied with the fruit of his mouth; with the increase of his lips shall he be filled. Death and life are in the power of the tongue; and they that love it shall eat the fruit thereof."* Proverbs 18:20 KJV

That was from the King James Version and I want to give you the text from two more versions, so you can get the full concept of the power that we have in our mouth. This is from the New Living Translation, and in verse 20 it says:

> *"Wise words satisfy like a good meal; the right words bring satisfaction. The tongue can bring death or life; those who love to talk will reap the consequences or the benefits."*
> Proverbs 18:20 NLT

I hope you're getting a concept of the power you have within you. The last text is from The Message Bible. These are different translations, but they give you a glimpse of the importance of utilizing proper words. In verse 20 again,

> *"Words satisfy the mind as much as fruit does the stomach; good talk is as gratifying as a good harvest. Words kill, words give life; they're either poison or fruit—you choose."*
> Proverbs 18:20 The Message

Remember this: death and life are truly in the power of your tongue. So, whose words are you using? How do you speak your own words? Are you speaking blessings or curses?

Don't Worry About Which Words To Use

Exodus 4:10–16 is the Scripture where you can read about the conversation between God and Moses where Moses is complaining to God that he is incapable of eloquent speech. I want to set in your mind and on your heart this reference to meditate on, to help you understand that we don't have to worry about what words to use when we speak. God is always going to provide resources, and the Holy Spirit is also there to guide us and to give us utterance in situations that we find ourselves. Let's look at Exodus 4:10,

> *"But Moses pleaded with the LORD, "O Lord, I'm just not a good speaker. I never have been, and I'm not now, even after you have spoken to me. I'm clumsy with words." "Who makes mouths?" the LORD asked him. "Who makes people so they can speak or not speak, hear or not hear, see or not see? Is it not I, the LORD? Now go, and do as I have told you. I will help you speak well, and I will tell you what to say.""*
> Exodus 4:10–12

Even with that, Moses was still complaining. And he said, *"But Moses again pleaded, "Lord, please! Send someone else." Exodus 4:13."* And the anger of the Lord was kindled against Moses because he was still being disobedient. We know this spirit within Moses cost him the dear price of not being able to set foot in the Promised Land—but he *was* given the opportunity to see it. His disobedience was present at the beginning when God called him. We know that even if we're not following the Word of God fully, we can still be used as an instrument of God. We can block our full blessings by not being able to see the Promised Land He has for us and to step foot in it—let me take that back. You'll be able to see it, but you won't be able to enjoy the fruit of that Promised Land. It says here,

> *"Then the LORD became angry with Moses. "All right," he said. "What about your brother, Aaron the Levite? He is a good speaker..."* Exodus 4:14

Even in his frailty and his unbelief, God could give Moses what he needed in the moment he needed it most, and God still provided a way for Moses to be used according to his calling. He asked,

> *"Then the LORD became angry with Moses. "All right," he said. "What about your brother, Aaron the Levite? He is a good speaker. And look! He is on his way to meet you now. And when he sees you, he will be very glad. You will talk to him, giving him the words to say. I will help both of you to speak clearly, and I will tell you what to do. Aaron will be your spokesman to the people, and you will be as God to him, telling him what to say." Exodus 4:14–16*

In this process, there's always a way, even when you're not in line with what you've been called to do or say. God has planned a way for you to become prosperous. We have to believe and have faith as the centurion did, faith in the Word of God. Those things that He decrees shall be just as He speaks them because He has ordained certain things to take place.

Let's look at Mark 11:21–24. This is something to keep in mind as you're mixing belief with faith in your prayers and guarding the words coming out of your mouth. This will give you an illustration and something to meditate on with regard to the power of the spoken word. It starts in verse 21 where Peter is speaking to Christ calling to His remembrance the fig tree that He'd cursed and how it had actually withered. So it says here,

> *"And Peter calling to remembrance said unto him, Master, behold, the fig tree which thou cursed is withered away. And Jesus answering said unto them, have faith in God. For verily I say unto you, that whatsoever ye shall say unto this mountain, Be thou removed, and be thou cast into the sea; and shall not doubt in his heart, but shall believe those things which he*

*saith shall come to pass; he shall have whatsoever he saith.
Therefore I say unto you, what things so ever ye desire, when
ye pray, believe that ye receive them, and ye shall have them."*
Mark 11:21–24 KJV

That reading is from the King James Version. We just want to leave you with it so that you can understand God is how and He is why you have creative power. You were born with it, gifted to it, and you have to use it to receive the blessings in this earthly realm that God has stored for you in the Heavens.

CHAPTER 10

PERFORM Segment

"In your majesty, ride out to victory, defending truth, humility, and justice. Go forth to perform awe-inspiring deeds!"

Psalm 45:4

We are now in our perform segment and the word *perform* equates with works in Scripture. From a practical everyday standpoint, business development in life is really our performance, and that's the key that makes all the difference in the world. It doesn't matter how good your business plan is. It doesn't matter how great your products are or how many years of experience you have had in your area of expertise. If you're not performing in a way that leads you to the results that you're looking for, then what you have is just a bunch of words on a piece of paper. It's not enough to just build a plan, nor is it enough to have great resources and folks who have the ability to put together concepts and organizations. It's not enough to talk about what you're going to do and how you're going to go about it.

You must add that additional element, which envelopes the whole concept of performance. The only way that you're going to see results is to perform—to *execute* is to *take action* is to *do*. These are the operative words as it relates to building your faith, your business, or anything that you do as it pertains to your interpersonal relationships. It's all about performance. How are you executing those things? How have they been outlined?

If we look at the Word of God throughout the Old Testament, as well as the New Testament, there are many places that address these performance words. There are also some actions that don't match those words. So, we have an opportunity to see our outcomes based on actions. The funny thing about action is that when you don't take action, that, in itself, is an action. It's not about the whole concept of being neutral. It's very difficult to be neutral because your inactivity has an outcome based on the fact that you should be performing, taking action, or doing something. When your operating plan dictates that you take an action and you don't do so, that also speaks to the outcome.

The concept of *success on God's terms* relates to what the performance is that God gives us and how it relates to our thought processes. How does it relate to the things that we're saying or the things that we say we believe about our business, about ourselves, our faith, our God, and about our interpersonal relationships? How we relate is a key element in being able to build and create. As we create in the image of God, recognizing Him as the ultimate Creator, we have to recognize that ability He has given us to be creative. Not only do we have to *say*, we have to put the activating power into *what* we say we believe about ourselves, our business, and about God, which really dictates how strong and what your performance will be.

Let's explore the Book of James 2:14–26. I'll quote text from two Bible versions to help you with the true understanding of these words. When we think about the Scripture outlined in James 2:14–26, the verse that most people think about is verse 20, *"Faith without works is dead."* People think about that when they start talking about faith and not taking action—that faith without works is dead. It's very important that you keep the words or the spiritual connotations that are in the Word in their proper context. I want you to read from the two different versions so that you get an up-to-date layman's view from The Message Bible's interpretation, which is very powerful. Then, the Amplified Bible is somewhat like a thesaurus in the sense that it gives you the synonyms of different words so that you can get the flavor of what it is being communicated. We've all heard the concept of faith without works being dead, but when we take a look at James, chapter 2, in the Amplified Bible, it reads:

"What is the use (profit), my brethren, for anyone to profess to have faith if he has no [good] works [to show for it]? Can [such] faith save [his soul]? If a brother or sister is poorly clad and lacks food for each day, And one of you says to him, Good-bye! Keep [yourself] warm and well fed, without giving him the necessities for the body, what good does that do? So also faith, if it does not have works (deeds and actions of obedience to back it up), by itself is destitute of power (inoperative, or dead). But someone will say [to you then], You [say you] have faith, and I have [good] works. Now you show me your [alleged] faith apart from any [good] works [if you can], and I by [good] works [of obedience] will show you my faith. You believe that God is one; you do well. So do the demons believe and shudder [in terror and horror such as to make a man's hair stand on end and contract the surface of his skin]! Are you willing to be shown [proof], you foolish (unproductive, spiritually deficient) fellow, that faith apart from [good] works is inactive and ineffective and worthless? Was not our forefather Abraham [shown to be] justified (made acceptable to God) by [his] works when he brought to the altar as an offering his [own] son Isaac? You see that [his] faith was cooperating with his works, and [his] faith was completed and reached its supreme expression [when he implemented it] by [good] works. And [so] the Scripture was fulfilled that says, Abraham believed

in (adhered to, trusted in, and relied on) God, and this was
accounted to him as righteousness (as conformity to God's
will in thought and deed), and he was called God's friend. You
see that a man is justified (pronounced righteous before God)
through what he does and not alone through faith [through
works of obedience as well as by what he believes]. So also
with Rahab the harlot—was she not shown to be justified
(pronounced righteous before God) by [good] deeds when she
took in the scouts and sent them away by a different route?
For as the human body apart from the spirit is lifeless,
so faith apart from [its] works of obedience is also dead."
James 2:14–26 AMP

So, when I read that in the Amplified Bible, it gave me a much clearer understanding of what was being communicated, apart from the King James Version, as it relates to the language used in that particular interpretation of Scripture. When we look at that same text in The Message Bible, which is written in everyday language, it's even more powerful as it relates to what's being communicated. I'm going through this exercise as an illustration so that when you are studying the Bible on your own, you can use it as a model to get the full meaning of what is being said in the text. Reading some versions may not give you the full flavor of what's being communicated. You can certainly read the NIV or some of the other translations, but I'm using this illustration, which I think is a very powerful illustration on this whole concept of faith without works being dead. The same text in The Message Bible reads:

"Dear friends, do you think you will get anywhere in this life
if you learn all the right words but never do anything? Does
merely talking about faith indicate that a person really has

it? For instance, you come upon an old friend dressed in rags and half-starved and say, "Good morning, friend! Be clothed in Christ! Be filled with the Holy Spirit!" and walk off without providing so much as a coat or a cup of soup—where does that get you? Isn't it obvious that God-talk without God-acts is outrageous nonsense? I can already hear one of you agreeing by saying, "Sounds good. You take care of the faith department, I'll handle the works department." Not so fast. You can no more show me your works apart from your faith than I can show you my faith apart from my works. Faith and works, works and faith, fit together hand in glove. Do I hear you professing to believe in the one and only God, but then observe you complacently sitting back as if you had done something wonderful? That's just great. Demons do that, but what good does it do them? Use your heads! Do not suppose for a minute that you can cut faith and works in two and not end up with a corpse upon your hands. Wasn't our ancestor Abraham "made right with God by works" when he placed his son Isaac on the sacrificial altar? Isn't it obvious that faith and works are yoked partners, that faith expresses itself in works? That the works are "works of faith"? The full meaning of "believe" in the Scripture sentence, "Abraham believed God and was set right with God," includes his action. It's that mesh of believing and acting that got Abraham named "God's friend." Is it not evident that a person is made right with God not by a barren faith but by a faith fruitful in works? The same with Rahab, the Jericho harlot. Wasn't her action in hiding God's spies and helping them escape—that seamless unity of believing and doing—what counted with God? The very moment you separate body and spirit, you end up with a corpse. Separate faith and works and you get the same thing: a corpse." James 2:14–26 The Message

This illustration and study gives us a deeper understanding of the words that are being communicated here and really helps us to understand that by simply believing you're going to be successful in your business or where you're going to work is not enough. Those things, without having a true relationship with God and without taking action, only demonstrate a false illustration of faith and show us that it's a dead faith. Your faith is illustrated in the actions that you take. Hebrews 11:1 says, *"What is faith? It is the confident assurance that what we hope for is going to happen. It is the evidence of things we cannot yet see."* How can you move forward in faith if you don't believe in the things you're hoping for? We can't always have tangible proof in front of us of the final outcome. Everything starts with the personal relationship you must build with God. Without Him, what would you have faith in? Who would bring those things to fruition? Having faith is absolutely believing in those things that aren't evident *yet*, but knowing in your heart they're on the horizon if you continue to work toward them. If you believe in God, you'll tithe, you'll take care of the homeless and the widows and the children and the orphans, and you'll have love for your fellow man, and you'll even pray for those who persecute you. This is a mandate spoken by God's Son, Jesus, to help us understand the way we gain a lot of the success we are privy to. We must understand that no man is an island unto himself. Do those things that are outlined in the Word of God, if you're really seeking to have everlasting success or success that will manifest itself in its most powerful way. Seek it the way God outlined it in His Word and you'll never go wrong. He is clearly saying to us that believing is one thing, but demons also believe there's a God and they tremble and shake in Jesus' presence, as we've read in Scripture (James 2:19). He successfully cast demons out of people in different stories in the Bible because He had radical faith that He knew how to put into action. So, believing is not enough. Having faith is a beautiful thing, but if you never take action, then you're not going to produce anything. Your faith is evident in the way that you treat people as well as in the way that you live your life on a day-to-day basis.

Your business is founded on the concept of relationships. Transactions take place through people who share these relationships. Even with a stranger, the purpose of advertising and coming up with eye-catching commercials is to create a relationship with the person watching, so that they can tie what they see into their feelings as it relates to how the product is being advertised. There's a trust factor involved here. If you turn on your television, the commercial is there. When you walk outside and look on the side of a bus, advertising is there. When you open a newspaper, you most likely find advertisements there as well, not to mention magazines, where you'll also find them. You see advertising when you go into a store or to a sporting event too. It builds trust that builds relationships between you and that company.

Your faith must be activated by the actions that you take with the people who are around you or in your center of influence. Through those relationships, trust and faith are activated. This shows through the actions that you take, through the words that you speak, and the thoughts that you have. If you don't understand what the thoughts of God are by reading what the Word of God says, then there's no way for you to thoroughly activate your faith through what's being said. You have to know for yourself what the Word of God says. You have to know for yourself what the intricate details are of your business plan and how you're going to execute them. This is a very key element to your success. Regardless of what the endeavors of your personal life are or your professional life, whatever it is that you're looking to do, believing is one thing, having faith is another thing, and it *all* shows up in your actions. If you show me what a person is doing, I can show you what they believe and what they're thinking. Your actions are a key element in your ability to create the success that you're looking for. If we're going to be creating success, we certainly want to be using the blueprint of the Creator and Founder of it all.

Serving Your Number One Asset: People

From a product standpoint as well as from a company standpoint, I want you to understand that products, companies, and your business, along with your compensation plans, are not nearly as important as your people. Not only does your success depend on having the right words, the right thoughts, and the right actions; it depends on your connection to the right people. We're talking about being able to serve people properly and, because we serve people properly, we can create outcomes and profits that facilitate the good success we are seeking.

So, as I was doing my studies, I realized that the word *perform* actually appears in Scripture 69 times. The words *performance* and *performing* appear twice. Performance simply means this: *To carry out, to accomplish with efficiency.* There are some outstanding synonyms that can really help you understand that when you have the right thoughts in mind and you speak the right words, then you can take the right actions. The results are wonderful because God is a pro-generator and He's called us to replicate, duplicate, dominate, to have dominion, power, infuse, and to absolutely take over. Here are some of the synonyms we think about when we hear the word *perform.* We're talking about words like achieve, act out, to execute, to function, to finish, to fulfill, to operate, to perk, to take care of business, to transact, to produce, to have production, to work, to bring to fruition, to deliver the goods, and also to have a functioning and active practice. I want to help you understand the opposite of a synonym, the *antonym.* Included in this category are words like fail, halt, prevent, or stop. The Scripture declares that God says, *"I am the Lord, the God of all the peoples of the world. Is anything too hard for me?"* (Jeremiah 32:27). So, when you understand that you have the ability to perform at the highest level, based on utilizing your gifts through the activity of creation that has been given to you, we have creative power to take action.

I want to demonstrate the power of the actions that we take or that we don't take and the consequences that we suffer when we don't. We all have the same potential. Now, we want to take that potential energy and that potential to create and make it kinetic by allowing it to manifest in the power we have to operate in the heavenly realm. One of the unique stories in the Bible is found in 1 Kings, chapter 17, where there was a prophet by the name of Elijah. Elijah was a powerful man and he was subject to our passions. The reason I chose Elijah is because some of you have brilliant ideas and some of you have had opportunities to expand and to impart to individuals. Sometimes we've had difficulties and we've chosen to listen to the voice that is contrary to what we've already done and to rely on our past experiences. Elijah was one of the most powerful prophets of his time and he had some significant power. As a matter of fact, he demonstrated his power by believing the Word of God and, in 1 Kings 17:1, he made a declaration. It says,

> *"Now Elijah, who was from Tishbe in Gilead, told King Ahab, "As surely as the Lord, the God of Israel, lives—the God I serve—there will be no dew or rain during the next few years until I give the word!""* 1 Kings 17:1

In other words, Elijah petitioned the Lord, and because he was having difficulty with Ahab and Ahab was always challenging the authority of God, through God he stopped all rainfall. I want you to understand, Ahab represents the enemy who's *always* challenging what God has already promised. Even in your past experiences, the success you have had is a reflection of what God will continue to do because He's the same yesterday, today, and forever. I want you to understand that sometimes when we have ideas, we have creative, witty ideas and sometimes we tend not to act on those or take action because we're in fear of it not coming to pass, but I want to assure you, according to the Word of God, that whatever God has given you to speak, if you follow through on what He's said, then guess what? It will come to pass. So, Elijah was instructed to, *"Go to the east and hide by Kerith Brook, near where it enters the Jordan River. "*

You may or may not be familiar with this verse of Scripture, but what ended up happening was a drought in the land. I want you to understand, although you have creative ideas, you may not have the financial resources, but because God has spoken it to you, if you obey His voice and do specifically what He tells you to do, God will sustain you, even when the circumstances and the environment are not conducive for you to produce. It's not actually because you're producing, but because He has the power to produce through you. Whatever He has told you to do, the Word of God encourages us to move forward in it and not be intimidated or afraid of the voice of the enemy. He said,

> *"Drink from the brook and eat what the ravens bring you, for I have commanded them to bring you food." So Elijah did as the Lord told him and camped beside Kerith Brook, east of the Jordan.* 1 King 17:4–5."

In other words, although what the Lord was telling him may not have made sense to Elijah at the time and he really may not have been able to see it because the circumstances weren't conducive, being that there was a drought, famine, and "recession", because he was instructed to act on the Word of God and he did so, he was provided for. Even in your current circumstances, you may not have the resources to build your business or to move forward the way you feel you need to, but Scripture says He will send the ravens.

So, what does this mean? It simply means that God will provide people who customarily would not come to your rescue or come to help you by any means, and because you are moving forward in action according to His Word in faith, He will supply your needs according to His riches and glory. He will always sustain you and allow you to participate in His ultimate plan when you're being obedient and acting according to His will. It's understandable that, because you have faith, as in this passage of Scripture, He will provide for you and keep you from falling prey to something or someone who is only thinking about themselves. We have ravens that are scavengers and are only concerned about feeding themselves, but because Elijah acted on the Word of God, he moved forward and was able to be sustained by those ravens, even in the famine and drought. If we do the same, God will sustain us as well. The Word says, beginning in verse 6 of chapter 17:

The ravens brought him bread and meat each morning and evening, and he drank from the brook. But after a while the brook dried up, for there was no rainfall anywhere in the land. Then the Lord said to Elijah, "Go and live in the village of Zarephath, near the city of Sidon. I have instructed a widow there to feed you." So he went to Zarephath. As he arrived at the gates of the village, he saw a widow gathering sticks, and he asked her, "Would you please bring me a little water in a cup?" As she was going to get it, he called to her, "Bring me a bite of bread, too." But she said, "I swear by the Lord your God that I don't have a single piece of bread in the house. And I have only a handful of flour left in the jar and a little cooking oil in the bottom of the jug. I was just gathering a few sticks to cook this last meal, and then my son and I will die." But Elijah said to her, "Don't be afraid! Go ahead and do just what you've said, but make a little bread for me first. Then use what's left to prepare a meal for yourself and your son. For this is what the Lord, the God of Israel, says: There will always be flour and olive oil left in your containers until the time when the Lord sends rain and the crops grow again!" So she did as Elijah said, and she and Elijah and her son continued to eat for many days. There was always enough flour and olive oil left in the containers, just as the Lord had promised through Elijah. 1 King 17:6–16

So folks, there is credence in the dynamics of your acting appropriately and being obedient to the Word of God. God will send you to a place and surround you with people, even in the midst of a famine when it seems that you don't have the natural resources to help you. He's the *super* in your *supernatural* and will always put you in a position where you can do His will and establish what He's purposed and destined for you to do.

Then, when we have a listening ear, when He tells us to move, guess what? Because of what you attempted to do while you were establishing your plan, your obedience is going to impact and affect the lives of everyone that you come in contact with. The widow woman was there in the drought for Elijah, as you heard the Word say. She was Elijah's "ram in the bush." God will always provide a way for you, even when you can't see one, when you're working according to His will.

This is the power that you have when you talk about starting your business to be a blessing, not only to yourself, but to the many people with whom you will communicate. As I stated previously, it is very important for you to act because your act of obedience will save the lives of the people who you care about the most, the people who exist in your families as well as the people who exist in your communities. So folks, it is very important for you to act in the purpose of establishing the foundation for the business that you have started, a business that will affect the Kingdom of God and the people who you reside with, in order to benefit them. Just by Elijah showing up and moving on the instruction God gave him, he was able to go to a place that was already prepared for him. The widow woman struggled because she was concerned about herself and her son, but at the same time, she understood and recognized the blessing that was before her, so she was obedient and acted as well, based on the Word that had been spoken to her.

This is what I really want to help you understand, that because of the obedience of Elijah speaking to that woman, and her obedience in reciprocating, we know that we are to replicate and duplicate their actions every day, because guess what happened folks? She and her son were sustained because she was obedient and because she acted on faith and the Word of God. Her works began to feed the man of God and, because of her obedience, she and her son were given the opportunity to live. The oil did not run out and the meal never ended, no matter how many times she dipped into the container. Through it all, little things became mighty big things. That small idea you may have, no matter what people may think of it, if it was given to you and if you've aligned yourself with the right thoughts by putting forth the right words and speaking the right things and performing the right actions, no matter where you are right now or how small the beginnings may be, never despise those small beginnings because they often lead to big things. You've been called, purchased and destined to create. You're supposed to help other people to expand and to be a blessing to those whom you've been sent to serve.

Chapter 11

—◦◦◦—

SEE Segment

"Christ is the one through whom God created everything in heaven and earth. He made the things we can see and the things we can't see—kings, kingdoms, rulers, and authorities. Everything has been created through him and for him."

Colossians 1:16

We've been exploring, over the last few chapters, this whole concept of how to think, speak, and perform to see the Kingdom of Heaven on earth. This chapter is about seeing the fruits of your labor; the *see* piece of the creation equation. We have discussed being able to have proper thoughts based on the Word of God and being able to proclaim those things from a verbal standpoint, then bringing them into the atmosphere where we can give vibration to those thoughts through your voice. There is the whole concept of performing. So, it's not enough to talk about the things that you desire or the things that you're working toward from a business development standpoint, you always have to take action. Another part of that equation is the ability to *see* the results of your efforts.

The funny thing about sight or the type of vision that is talked about in Scripture is that a lot of times you have to see it before you can actually bring it to fruition. Seeing something prior to taking action gives you the ability to see it in reality. There's a cliché some use that goes, *"I'll believe it when I see it,"* but people who really understand how the creation equation works see it first, which allows them to believe it. They see it first in a special way! They see in their minds the vision or the possibilities of a desired outcome. You have to see yourself in that final state of success. As you allow the thoughts of God to work on your behalf and line up your speech patterns and actions with His, you begin to receive the ability to see the outcome before it manifests itself in the world, so to speak. It gives you the ability to continue performing, even when your eyes are telling you that what you're working toward is not going to happen. Even when your ears are hearing pessimistic statements, because of people doubting and giving you negative feedback by saying things like: *"Oh, that's not going to work", "You're wasting your time", "Why don't you find something else to do?", "Why are you studying for a degree when there are no jobs out there?", "Why are you working an extra job? You should be at home doing things you need to do with your family and just sacrifice the well being"* and, *"Why are you doing that network marketing business?"*

You have to press on. People will try to bring doubt into the equation, but God has already manifested your vision in Heaven and dropped it into the earth for you to bring life to it in the natural. This whole concept of seeing or having vision is definitely key.

Throughout the New Testament, Scripture talks about Christ giving sight to the blind. In some of those instances, it wasn't so much the physical aspect of whether or not a person could see with their physical eyes. If you really study some of those instances, they were talking about people being blind to the Kingdom of God here on earth or blind to the ability to manifest it or even see it as it was represented in Christ Jesus. They were blind! They didn't know that the Kingdom of God had come to earth through the person of Jesus the Christ. They were blind to that. They were actually walking around with their eyes wide shut. The fact that Jesus was able to help the blind to see as one of His miracles, through the things that He was able to show them in a physical sense, also allowed them to see true manifestation of God in the flesh through Jesus and to experience the Kingdom of Heaven on earth.

The whole concept of sight, of seeing is multifaceted in the sense that it's not just about being able to see with your physical eye, but it's also about having vision—being able to see with your eyes closed. If you can see with your eyes closed, then with them closed add prayer and return the Word of God to God. He is looking for you to bring His Word to remembrance. The whole concept of remembrance is not about memory, but about bringing the Word of God back to God in a way that He can begin to operate in the supernatural for you. As you pray in your natural voice using spiritual words, the words of God, and pray in a way that tells Him you understand that He's made promises in His Word throughout Scripture, you are resonating those promises back to Him. There's an agreement, in a sense, that these are promises made and promises being brought back together through the Word. Therefore, you have an opportunity to see these things with your eyes closed while offering prayer that gives you the ability to see through your natural eye those things supernaturally manifested. When you do this, your spiritual eyes are opened. What-ever that goal is for your business, if you have milestones, as they relate to revenue, you have to operate in a fashion that gives you the ability to manifest the outcome even before the outcome manifests itself. You have to have belief, faith, and performance to speak those things that are not as though they were, as it pertains to speaking them into existence.

Our Scriptural reference for this particular segment speaks to this whole concept of vision. In Proverbs 29:18 KJV there's a simple statement, *"Where there is no vision, the people perish; but he that keepeth the law, happy is he."* The law is the Word of God and as you keep that spiritual law that He has dictated in His Word, you are given the opportunity to understand what God sees for us. The type of life that He sees for us speaks to abundance, overflow, and having no wants because all of our needs are met through our ability to line up with creation as He has fashioned it. It gives us the ability to receive what the Scripture describes as happiness in Proverbs 29:18. Then, we have the Book of Habakkuk, chapter 2, verse 2. Habakkuk is one of those books that not many people even know is in the Bible. I know the first time I heard this particular Scripture quoted, I was, like, *"Is that an actual book in the Bible?"* Habakkuk is in the Old Testament and chapter 2, verse 2 says:

> *"And the Lord answered me and said write the vision and engrave it so plainly upon tablets that everyone who passes may [be able to] read [it easily and quickly] as he hastens by."*
> Habakkuk 2:2 AMP

This is from the Amplified Version of the Bible, which gives a deeper interpretation of the Word. If we look at the King James Version, it simply states,

> *"And the Lord answered me, and said, write the vision and make it plain upon tables, that he may run that readeth it."*
> Habakkuk 2:2 KJV

So, when the vision is clear, it's very easy to execute in the way you need to execute in order to reach the outcome you're working toward, whether it's in a personal relationship or a business relationship—whatever the case may be. You have an opportunity to understand what you're working toward and seeing it gives more credence to your mind while giving you confidence to proceed. It gives you faith to perform that which allows you to continue to perform until you see the goal you're working to achieve manifested.

It might take you a year to achieve the goal that you've set. In those first six months, you might not be able to see any physical results of your efforts, but if you can keep that vision locked in internally and continue to perform, you'll have the opportunity to see those things manifested in the earthly realm and to produce something that you can actually see with your physical eyes—that "evidence not seen" finally showing itself.

Right now, you are reading this book and you're probably sitting in a chair or leaning on a counter, or maybe you're in a room surrounded by four walls with light fixtures and furniture. Everything that we see started out as an idea in someone's mind at some point, a vision or something in their imagination, but definitely as something that they were looking to create. The blueprint for your home or apartment started in an architect's mind. Then, it went onto paper as a blueprint and, later, someone took hammers, nails, plaster, plywood, and sheetrock in order to make it a reality. The manifestation of it took place. Although in the beginning, it was just an idea. I don't know who created the first chair, but at some point it was the first chair ever created. I don't know who perfected the wheel, but at some point it was the first wheel and just an idea in someone's mind, created to serve a purpose or a need. So, although we see these things with our physical eyes now, people envisioned the things that we're wearing and the page that you are reading in their minds *first*. They all started out as a drawing, just an idea in someone's mind. There was some need that manifested and created the desire to invent a phone, TV, laptop, tape, your shoes, an IPod, or whatever item you choose. At some point, it was an internal vision that manifested in a physical way. God is saying to us as He admonishes us to read, study, and meditate on His Word for ourselves that we should allow that Word to resonate and manifest itself on the things He's promised us.

A lot of times, we stop and start, stop and start, we study and we don't study, we go to church and then we don't go to church, we listen and we're obedient, and then we don't listen and we're disobedient, we go back and forth, teetering and tottering, and learning through our experiences when everything has been all laid out in the sixty-six books of the Holy Bible by Almighty God, who is waiting for us to be obedient and take action on the vision He has prepared for each of us.

Know for Yourself

I remember being on a call with someone who was talking about the Bible and they used the letters of the word *Bible* as an acronym, Basic Instructions Before Leaving Earth or BIBLE. Before we can leave from where we are and make it to the next level, we have to learn to follow the instructions that are in the Scriptures. The Bible is an instruction manual written through the prophets by the Creator. If you want to check on how to use a product, you read the instruction manual that comes with it. With mankind being a product of God, if you want to check with anyone regarding *us* as a product, it makes sense to me that you check with the Creator to understand how to operate in the triune nature of your being, whether that be in the physical, the spiritual, or the mental/emotional aspect of your being. Our spirit, that part of God that lives in us, and our soul control our emotions, intellect, and will, along with our physical body. So, there are three things happening inside of us as part of our being at all times. We have this triune nature that we have to manage and He shares with us just how to do that through His Word.

Success on God's terms is found in the Scriptures and you have to get to know them for yourself. It's one thing for someone to preach a sermon to you, but it's another thing for you to live and experience it for yourself. It's one thing for someone to pray for you, but it is a whole new experience if you're praying for yourself and others. You have to experience things for yourself and be able to recognize when things manifest themselves in your life. You have to get to know the foundation that's been set and that is only found in the thoughts of God, which are captured in the Word of God.

Supernatural Vision

It is absolutely awesome when you get to the point where you under-stand how critical sight is and how important it is to the dynamics of where you are. I just want to highlight the purpose of your sight and just how critical it is to you. I want to share a couple of defini-tions with you because everything that we have has been revealed in Scripture through the Word of God and He's placed it upon the fleshy parts of our hearts. There's a GPS, a global positioning system, designed inside of each of us to direct us to the path on which He has already called us. This was one of the purposes of the Incarnation of Jesus in the flesh, that man would no longer have to teach us, but during that time period, God's Word would be written on the fleshy parts of our hearts. So, there's something in us that will drive us to the point of wanting to understand His purpose for us.

Success on God's terms is a phrase that you may be familiar with, but I want to give you a different perspective on it because, truly we are *a* light but, without *the* Light, nothing can be seen. You have to understand that, because you have the Light, the scales will fall from your eyes so that you will be able to see through your spiritual eyes and understand the word that we call *illumination*. It's like peering at something with a bright light on. At first, it displays like it's under a 40 watt light bulb, but when you put that fluorescent light on it, then you have a brighter understanding and a better view of what is already in existence. According to Ephesians 2:6, the Word of God declares that because of the relationship we have from being birthed into the right family, we will sit together in the heavenly places. In the King James Version, it says He, *"hath raised us up together, and made us sit together in the heavenly places in Christ Jesus."* So, where you and I are concerned, because of the proper sight you have, you're al-ready seated in heavenly places. You have the right perspective, being able to see every obstacle that you may face and every obstacle that may threaten your business because you have the right focal point, a special 20/20 vision, so you are able to see past that initial stage of development. It's like putting your hand close to your face; you know your hand is there, but you can't see it because you don't have the proper perspective yet. As you move that hand further and further away from your face, pretty soon you are able to identify what it is. That's similar to what they say about a child when he or she is first born. They can only see blurry images. What we want to be able to do, because the Word of God glows so bright, is to allow it to shine a light on our path and direct us. It will warn us, move us, help us partner in the right relationships, and help us endure until we reach the end result.

Let's look over in 2 Corinthians at the fourth chapter, starting in verse 5. The text illustrates how important it is to have the right perspective on who you truly are. As we are building and establishing the Kingdom of Heaven on earth, we are already seated in the heavenly places. As you think of this in the natural, you may think of the royal family in England. Just because they were born into the right family, they already have privileges that the average citizen does not have. They have advantages that average citizens will never have, simply because average citizens were not born into this type of royal family. However, if we can maintain proper vision and continue seeing the end from the beginning, we'll be able to navigate through the process, engaging in personal relationships and working hard on business relationships, because the end result has already been pre-determined. That's good news for you and me and I want to help you understand why. When you read 2 Corinthians, chapter 4 verses 5 thru 18 in the New Testament, it simply says that,

> "We don't go around preaching about ourselves; we preach Christ Jesus, the Lord. All we say about ourselves is that we are your servants because of what Jesus has done for us. For God, who said, "Let there be light in the darkness," has made us understand that this light is the brightness of the glory of

God that is seen in the face of Jesus Christ. But this precious treasure—this light and power that now shine within us—is held in perishable containers, that is, in our weak bodies. So everyone can see that our glorious power is from God and is not our own. We are pressed on every side by troubles, but we are not crushed and broken. We are perplexed, but we don't give up and quit. We are hunted down, but God never abandons us. We get knocked down, but we get up again and keep going. Through suffering, these bodies of ours constantly share in the death of Jesus so that the life of Jesus may also be seen in our bodies. Yes, we live under constant danger of death because we serve Jesus, so that the life of Jesus will be obvious in our dying bodies. So we live in the face of death, but it has resulted in eternal life for you. But we continue to preach because we have the same kind of faith the psalmist had when he said, "I believed in God, and so I speak." We know that the same God who raised our Lord Jesus will also raise us with Jesus and present us to himself along with you. All of these things are for your benefit. And as God's grace brings more and more people to Christ, there will be great thanksgiving, and God will receive more and more glory. That is why we never give up. Though our bodies are dying, our spirits are being renewed every day. For our present troubles are quite small and won't last very long. Yet they produce for us an immeasurably great glory that will last forever! So we don't look at the troubles we can see right now; rather, we look forward to what we have not yet seen. For the troubles we see will soon be over, but the joys to come will last forever" 2 Corinthians 4:5–18

Although it is not apparent, the equation of creation starts with what we see within ourselves. We are faced with the same trials and tribulations, and when it comes to you, you may be in a situation where you don't have the necessary financial resources, but realize this: because you've been birthed into the right family, you are a son or daughter of the King, so you have everything you need at your disposal. Those obstacles that appear before you—the naysayers, the doubters, the people who come to steal your dreams—they don't realize the visions that were *birthed* in you and it's just a matter of you understanding them yourself, according to Matthew chapter 16 verses 18 and 19, where it says, *"Truly the gates of hell shall not prevail against you."* And the Lord Jesus says, *"I'll give you the keys to the Kingdom."*

This means you have all the power and the authority to operate and walk out your dream according to what has been purposed for your life, but it's all about what you continuously focus on and what you see on a day-to-day basis. With this supernatural vision, you are able to see through the darkest circumstances in your life, when the enemy tries to take you through your darkest calamity.

When you keep your eyes on the Light of the world, He will help you reach the understanding that you have laser-sharp vision and the ability to see beyond what is visible in the natural world. You have this vision because of the creative power you are able to perceive through the knowledge that you are seated in heavenly places. You have the power to look through that thick wall or that thick obstacle because it's just a mirage. When it appears to be something that's going to cause you to stumble, because you have supernatural x-ray vision, you have the ability to diminish it and call it out. What you say will be based on what you see, for things have to be seen before they can be manifested. Once you see it, you can speak and rebuke any enemy that tries to stop your progress. We're removing the scales from your eyes, so you're no longer blinded—you can operate using that supernatural vision.

It does not matter what has happened (or has not happened) as long as you have the understanding that Light overcomes the darkest dark. Because you have the Light, you have the ability to move forward in the light, visualizing your future.

Facts About your Eyes

There are a couple of things about your eyes that are very interesting. When I was in biology class, the instructor informed us that our eyes really see images upside down, but our brain reverses the images. The fact that we have two eyeballs gives us the ability to have three-dimensional vision and it gives us perspective. Our eyes work in sync, but the images that we see are really upside down and our brain switches them, so that we get the proper perspective from a physical standpoint.

The thing about our physical realm is that it's not always what it seems. It's all about perspective, perception, and experience. Have you ever been looking for something and you're looking all over the place trying to find it? Then, you find what you're looking for in a place that you'd already looked, but you didn't see it the first time you searched that place? The thing about our brain is that it's designed to filter out stimuli that we are not focusing on. It allows us to focus on a few things at a time. If we were processing every single sound and everything that our eyes actually detected and relayed to our brains, this would overwhelm us. So, our brain helps us filter things out. If I told you right now to stand where you are in your house and look around the room and do a 360-degree turn slowly, picking out everything that is black in your room, you would turn around focusing on everything black. My TV monitor is black, I have a suit right there that is black, a desk, I've got a pouch right there and my briefcase. My brain is saying, *"Okay, I'm going to pick up all the things that are black."* The hanger is black and the cords on my power cord to the laptop are black. So, if I ask you to pick out everything black but then, once you'd done that, I say to you, *"Now tell me everything that was orange,"* you probably wouldn't be able to tell me because you weren't focused on that color. You were focusing on what was black. Even though your eyes picked up things that were orange or blue or another color, your brain didn't process those colors. The thing about physical sight is that it can be deceiving or might not be able to give you all the information that you need in a given instant.

That's why you have to anchor your sight and your vision in God's vision. His vision is perfect. His vision and what He wants for your life are perfect. If you just align yourself with Him, close your eyes, put your hands over your ears, and go inside (where you have the Word of God anchored, because you meditate on it day and night, speak it, and read it), it won't matter what your eyes are telling you. It *shouldn't* matter what other people are saying, if you're focused on the Word of God. If you're focused on the promises that He's made for you, then you can get those things He's promised because His Word is perfect.

The thing about His Word is that it also tells you what's going to happen if you *don't* follow it. Feigning ignorance is not a disclaimer. There are people out there operating without the knowledge of God's Word. They're executing the spiritual laws and seeing results while serving someone else, but they're still using the spiritual laws. God also talks about those people who are not following the Word of God the way it's described, as it relates to what the outcome will be in their situation. You can close your eyes and your ears and still recognize, if you focus on the vision that God has for your life, what He has stored up for you and you should just walk in that. Think those thoughts, speak those words, and perform those actions and you will be able to see with your physical eye those things He's promised. Now, some of those things are brought about in a day, some in a month, and some are going to manifest in a year. Some may take ten years while some things may take twenty years to manifest. It might even take you thirty years to get that thing He promised, but the idea is that God's timing is always perfect. You might think you need it at year twenty, but He's saying it's perfect for you at year thirty. You just have to keep pressing forward, keep looking for what's manifesting by doing the things you need to do.

So, sight is a dual thing. We can't allow our physical senses to deceive us on a spiritual level. We can't allow our eyes to deceive us about the vision that God has for us. We can't allow our physical bodies to control the process, nor our emotions or intellect, when the Word of God is perfect and sure. His Word will never return void, as is described in Scripture. You have to believe in those things and have faith. Then again, it's not enough to believe and have faith; you have to perform and you have to take action. Those heavenly things that God talks about will give you an opportunity to see the Kingdom of Heaven on earth.

PART 3

Occupy Until the Return

CHAPTER 12

─◈─

The Kingdom of Heaven on Earth

"May your Kingdom come soon. May your will be done here on earth, just as it is in heaven."

Matthew 6:10

*L*ooking at the Word of God, we recognize that commentary about Heaven and earth is prevalent throughout Scripture. Genesis opens up with descriptions of Heaven and the firmament. In Genesis 2:7 KJV, it says:

> *"And the Lord God formed man of the dust of the ground, and breathed into his nostrils the breath of life. And man became a living soul."*

I want you to reflect on that Scripture for a moment because I'm going to come back to this at the conclusion of this chapter. This Bible verse is key to this conversation of the Kingdom of Heaven on earth and what it means in a spiritual as well as a physical context.

We know by looking at Scripture in Genesis that the creation equation is described clearly and it appears very early. The way this is emphasized starts in the first sentence, where it says, *"In the beginning God created the heavens and earth"* (Genesis 1:1). So, the whole concept of Heaven and earth are present from the onset of the story that unfolds in Scripture. We are here on the earth toiling, learning, growing, and we're going through our trials and tribulations as outlined in the Word of God. We know, certainly, the Word of God does not return void, so in His Word He's already described to us the things that will transpire as we allow that living soul within us to mature. As it matures, we are in a constant battle to bring the Kingdom of Heaven to the earthly realm.

I want you to stop and think about something. It may take a little imagination for you to think about what I'm communicating in regard to the Kingdom of Heaven on earth. Look in Genesis where it reads, *"And God called the firmament heaven. And the evening and the morning were the second day."* That's Genesis 1:8 KJV.

"And God said, let the waters under the heaven be gathered unto one place, and let the dry land appear; and it was so"
Genesis 1:9 KJV

" And God said, let there be lights in the firmament of the heaven to divide the day from the night; and let them be for signs, and for seasons, and for days, and for years."
Genesis 1:14 KJV

God dictated what all of this would mean to us as it relates to our lives here on earth. When you look at this next verse, *"And let them be for lights in the firmament of the heaven to give light upon the earth; and it was so"* (Genesis 1:15), we are brought to the realization that at the very beginning creation was *spoken* into existence, unfolding God's story of His Son, Jesus Christ.

Note that we have been made from the earth. The Scripture regarding the breath of life from Genesis 2:7 KJV reads:

> *"And the Lord God formed man of the dust of the ground, and breathed into his nostrils the breath of life. And man became a living soul."*

This the beginning of our very existence. Our bodies were formed from the ground and we are actually living earth. We each have a living soul, but the Spirit of God is within us and animates the earth that our body is made of. If you think about it just from a conceptual standpoint, every part of our physical body comes from the earth, as does the food that we eat. From the standpoint of eating meat, the flesh of a cow or chicken we consume as a meal also eats things of the earth. Every part of our body is made up of the same components as the earth. This whole concept of Heaven and earth, in my simple equation, is that God wants to live in all of us. He wants to bring those spiritual thoughts into a physical vibration. Then, as we speak through our physical body, the elements begin to respond to us. The time frame for those things to manifest is irrelevant because time is really an illusion. We have to allow God to live in us. He wants to live in us; He wants to live in the earth and have dominion *over* the earth that we represent as we walk out our purposes day by day. Because God completely resides in you, you stop fighting Him so much, even in your sin and disobedience, making it possible for you to possess your promised physical land completely. You can possess your promised, living, animated earth companion in the person of your wife or your husband. You can take care of your living, animated, earth descendants, and leave a spiritual inheritance for your offspring. Those people that we call our sons and our daughters are made up of the same DNA that we are made of. We combine that DNA with our companion and have offspring. In the concept of the apple not falling far from the tree, if God is living in us and we are manifesting His Kingdom through our possessions, our thoughts, and our physical possessions; then, those children who are part of our lineage will be subject to the same things within us.

We have the opportunity to allow God to live within us and, as we allow Him to grow in us, His Kingdom is established in the earth through us. As we allow God to live in us, His Kingdom is established in the earth—a kingdom that we represent through our physical bodies. Now that Spirit, who dwells in heavenly places begins to dwell in us. He begins to take over that living soul that He animated with various emotions, will, and intellect that He created as part of us. Ultimately, our soul starts being guided by the Spirit who comes from Heaven. We learn about the heavenly places that bring heavenly thoughts as those things begin to dictate what will happen through us. Only then can we begin to have the type of Godly success that our Father has laid out and stored up for us.

We now have an opportunity, through our actions, our thoughts, and by allowing things to line up with God who resides within us, to establish the Kingdom of Heaven here on earth. Only then can we occupy until He returns. We occupy through our daily tasks, through our thoughts and our actions, and we learn to sustain ourselves, from our livelihoods to the interactions that we have in our inter-personal and business relationships. Our Kingdom is established wherever we go. There God is—wherever we are. God is there with us because He's living in us and His kingdom can be established on every inch of ground that our feet tread upon. This means that, as people enter your presence, they are able to sense that the Kingdom of God is there and that He resides within you. So, if you really want to be able to see things manifested in your life, you simply have to think the thoughts and speak the Word of God. You have to perform the actions that are prescribed in His Word and then God will dwell in you in a very powerful way. As you align yourselves with Him, you open yourselves to create a space of righteousness for Him to dwell in. Doing that gives you the opportunity to manifest those things of God here in the earthly realm. Each of us is a vessel He can use.

So, God can live in the earth in the person of you, His living, animated, earth, and there's no debate about the origin of your body. It is Scriptural and the scientific community is beginning to accept this as well, that we all come from the earth that we walk on. In order for us to see the Kingdom of God manifested in the earth that we are, God has to reside in us. We can see this whole concept again in Revelation 21:1-3. It reads;

> *"And I saw a new heaven and a new earth; for the first heaven and the first earth were passed away; and there was no more sea."* Revelation 21:1 KJV

There will no longer be a division (sea). The first heaven and the first earth will eventually pass away, only to be replaced by an eternal city that surpasses anything our imagination can create. The sea will no longer exist, but rivers of water will flow from the throne of God and Jesus. Verse 2 says,

> *"And I John saw the holy city, New Jerusalem, coming down from God out of heaven, prepared as a bride adorned for her husband."* Revelation 21:2 KJV

This is the whole concept of the marriage covenant, two becoming one, heaven and earth becoming one. Verse 3 reads,

> *"And I heard a great voice out of heaven saying, Behold, the tabernacle of God is with men, and he will dwell with them, and they shall be his people, and God himself shall be with them, and be their God."* Revelation 21:3 KJV

God wants to dwell *in* you and *with* you and to get rid of the separation that was created by the first Heaven and the first earth. He has created a holy city that will replace the old city and God is coming down out of Heaven to unite with us here on earth. We have been created in the earth from earth, but for those of us who strive to overcome the wiles of the enemy through the enmity of the soul and body, a new city and eternal life awaits us.

So, that's my story and I'm sticking to it, and it's really His story. You are earth and God wants to live in you. You are living, animated, earth and, in order for the Kingdom of God to manifest here on earth, He has to dwell in you.

The Book of Ezra

It is a tremendous blessing to understand that the essence of what we want to share with you in this book is found and rooted in the blueprint, the Bible, which gives us the foundation for what we're talking about.

In the very beginning of the Bible, we were instructed to replicate and show what earth looks like from a heavenly perspective. Of course, we've been assigned and admonished to do that. I want to share with you some relevant things from the Book of Ezra. It gives insight around the responsibilities that we have in our day-to-day activities as we build our businesses and in the lives of people who have been assigned to us. While we are actively creating and training protégé's, we should be imparting into other people's lives so that we can see the manifestation of God on the earth, as we think proper things, speak proper words, and take the proper actions to perform.

My challenge to you is for you to think about how many people you've replicated yourself in. Have you duplicated yourself? As you take on your assignment, there's going to be a greater perpetuation of how the Kingdom will be established. We've been uniquely designed and we've been called out because, in order for the true manifestation of Heaven to be reflected on earth, each and every one of has to be in sync and prepared to do their part.

I just want to share with you from the Book of Ezra, chapter 1. Before the time period of Ezra, Solomon had established the tabernacle, the place where God would dwell. The Glory of the Lord would be there. Sometimes, we get out of order and become disobedient to the game plan and the guidelines. Then we lose order, which causes us to lose influence. These are some of the challenges that we face as business owners, where we disengage from that initial blueprint and have to be led into captivity for making unwise business decisions (decisions that were unwise because we didn't seek wise counsel). So, here in the Book of Ezra, we see that Ezra the prophet was given the opportunity to reestablish or begin the process of rebuilding the Kingdom. As we're thinking about our own individual businesses, we must understand that we still have an opportunity, no matter where we started, to rebuild. That is what our responsibility is. It reads in Ezra:

> *"In the first year of King Cyrus of Persia, the LORD fulfilled Jeremiah's prophecy by stirring the heart of Cyrus to put this proclamation into writing and to send it throughout his kingdom: "This is what King Cyrus of Persia says: The LORD, the God of heaven, has given me all the kingdoms of the earth. He has appointed me to build him a Temple at Jerusalem in the land of Judah. All of you who are his people may return to Jerusalem in Judah to rebuild this Temple of the LORD, the God of Israel, who lives in Jerusalem. And may your God be with you!." Ezra 1:1–3*

As we're looking at this information and working toward establishing a foundation in the Kingdom, there's an expectancy of establishing a city of peace and a city of refuge that God can dwell in. Ultimately, this is the reflection of seeing what Heaven on earth really represents. It represents the harmony, the peace of God in our businesses, the attraction because of His Spirit being there, with all parts working together and attracting others collectively. It's like having a magnet pulling at us and, because the magnet is so strong, all the separated pieces come together to make a complete picture. Look at the responsibility you have in your local community. The businesses you're planning have an impact on everyone there—we have a responsibility to build in a way that is going to bring peace and allow us to get back to the original plan that was intended for you and me.

Our whole plan and purpose is to establish the presence, the Kingdom, the rule, the authority, and the power of God in the earth. Once we establish the authority and the power, then our responsibility is to attract people and impart His gifts to them so that we can pour out more of Him. We can build using one block, one brick, one person at a time, and create protégés and images reflective of the initial state in which we existed, and we do so in order to bring it to fruition because we are already seated in heavenly places. We're extending our funnel of faith to pull down Heaven so that we can see it on earth. We no longer have to wait for the place that we're going to because it can exist in our very presence, even in times when people seem to be stressed out, and even in this state of so-called economic recession.

I'll leave you with this. As we talk about Heaven, what is Heaven? Heaven is a state of mind, a state of being. The definition says *"it's a place or state of supreme happiness; an eternal state of communion; a condition or place of great happiness, delight or pleasure."* So, your responsibility as a business builder, a Kingdom dweller, and as a person looking to see the manifestation of Heaven on earth is to do God's will as it's so eloquently said in Matthew, chapter 6:9–10:

> *"Our Father in heaven, may your name be honored. May your Kingdom come soon. May your will be done here on earth, just as it is in heaven..."* Matthew 6:9–10

So, we're looking to establish sweet serenity and be in a state of perpetual peace as we build our businesses and mentor people because every asset that we have was given to us by our Creator and prime benefactor, God. God expects a rate of return on His investment in us, not only from a financial standpoint, but from a discipleship standpoint, where we're constantly affecting the lives of the people who we interact with.

I want to remind you that we have a responsibility to share, and the more we share, the more we will see the Kingdom of Heaven on earth. Ultimately, God loved us so much that He wanted to see harmony on earth because the earth had become chaotic. He sent His only Son, Christ Jesus, into the earthly realm to reconcile all things back unto Himself. Therefore, we must be able to position people to receive the eternal gift of God, which allows us to have eternal peace because we have been made whole with God through Jesus the Christ. This helps our businesses to flourish and allows us think, see, perform, and take action to see the Kingdom of Heaven on earth.

CHAPTER 13

—⚬⚬⚬—

God Can Use You

"For God knew his people in advance, and he chose them to become like his Son, so that his Son would be the firstborn, with many brothers and sisters. And having chosen them, he called them to come to him. And he gave them right standing with himself, and he promised them his glory. What can we say about such wonderful things as these? If God is for us, who can ever be against us?"

Romans 8:29–31

This chapter is about you. The simple fact is, regardless of where you are now in your walk with God through Jesus, *God can use you.*

As humans, we experience those things we believe in, things we unconsciously have faith in as we go through our everyday activities. We eat in restaurants, we order food from fast food places, we drive in cars that we did not build, we use other products that we didn't create, and we just have faith—we assume that these things will perform the function that they were designed to perform. We deal with people who are in our families who have been in our lives and we just have faith that things and people are going to perform the way that they have been designed or purposed to. In the process of faith, we also walk around with fears, unspoken fears about our past, our present, about our future. Sometimes, this fear limits the things that

God can do through us and for us. In this concept of limiting, what really happens is that we place limits on our belief. So, fear leads to doubts, doubts lead to limiting beliefs, limiting beliefs lead to compromise, and compromise eventually leads to guilt in some form or fashion. Because we end up with this guilt, we sometimes feel that we're not worthy. We don't feel worthy of *success on God's terms* or even on our own (or someone else's) terms. You don't feel like you're worthy and you can't be used by God.

We have a very simple message about the fact that God *can* use you. He can even use you in your current state, regardless of what you feel that is, because He's not looking at it the way that you're looking at it. He's measuring the contents of your heart. He's measuring your intentions and those things that He's put in you and purposed in you since the beginning of time. Throughout Scripture people have been used who felt like they wouldn't be a candidate for God's work. Moses carried guilt because he was charged with murder. He had a speech impediment, which he felt gave him a lack of ability to communicate with others effectively. Even with that, there was provision made through his brother, Aaron. Yes, Moses was a murderer, but he was used by God. We know that Rahab was a prostitute but she helped the spies Joshua sent into the Promised Land, and she was one of the great grandmothers of Jesus, our Savior. Certainly, once God started using them, you wouldn't have known she had been a prostitute or wouldn't have recognized Moses as a person with a speech impediment. Throughout the Bible, the dejected, the slaves, the unlikely people have been used for the purposes of advancing the Kingdom of God and allowing the stories to unfold as God would have them.

Wherever you are right now, in your current walk, your current state, you can be used by God to bless others as well as yourself. So, be encouraged—the story is not over. It's continuing to be written. The acts of God are prevalent throughout today. His mercy and grace are apparent because, beyond the shadow of a doubt, we had a death sentence waiting for us, but we're saved by the shedding of the blood of Christ Jesus for the remission of our sins and the redemption that He provided for us—this is the spiritual law that has been set forth by the Word of God. There was a provision made for us and it's being made on a daily basis. Someone out there needs what you have. Put yourself in a position where you can be a blessing to those who cross your path. Even if it's for something as simple as a smile or a nickel you could lend or a word of encouragement to someone who needs it—that's a blessing. If you give of your time or do a selfless act or benefit someone, even if it means you will never see the end result of your action, you have planted a seed. Work on planting a very strong seed in a person who needs what you have to offer at that time, especially if they know that it was given out of a genuine heart, out of a genuine act of love.

Sharing the love of God with people who are in your sphere of influence brings you into the path of folks who may never know that you wanted to bless them and those blessings will come back a hundredfold for a harvest that can be reaped. We're all connected, we all have impact, and we all have to take the appropriate actions to be a blessing, recognizing that we do have something to offer the world, understanding that we cannot allow perceptions or feelings of guilt and unworthiness to keep us from being that blessing to someone else or allow things to deter us from pursuing the heart and mind of God through Christ Jesus.

We must understand that, in our imperfection, we are truly being perfected by God. We have to realize that our responsibility is to submit our will to God the Father through His Son, Christ Jesus. Through the heart of Jesus is where we can see our inadequacies and our shortcomings. It is here that we must allow our *natural* to be combined with the *supernatural* in the Spirit of God. The thing to know is the thing that Paul says to the Philippians:

> *"And I am sure that God, who began the good work within you, will continue his work until it is finally finished on that day when Christ Jesus comes back again."* Philippians 1:6

Be at peace where you are right now in your personal life as well as your business life. It's ultimately the responsibility of God to take you and mold you into that vessel of honor that He would have you to be. When we realize that, we know God is not surprised at where we are. It's all been preordained. It's been on His mind what he wants you and I to continually be.

The luxury that you and I have, as we've committed and submitted our lives to God the Father through Christ Jesus, is that, even while He's molding and making us, there's a great peace that comes when we understand that we're really in the best place possible, being with Him. In order for us all to understand what we were created to be, we must go to the individual, the person, the Creator of all creation to get the direct correlation of what we've been designed to be. Instruction was given to Jeremiah in 18:1–11, where it says:

> *"The LORD gave another message to Jeremiah. He said," Go down to the shop where clay pots and jars are made. I will speak to you while you are there." So I did as he told me and found the potter working at his wheel. But the jar he was making did not turn out as he had hoped, so the potter squashed the jar into a lump of clay and started again. Then the LORD gave me this message: "O Israel, can I not do to you as this potter has done to his clay? As the clay is in the potter's hand, so are you in my hand. If I announce that a certain nation or kingdom is to be uprooted, torn down, and destroyed, but then that nation renounces its evil ways, I will not destroy it as I had planned. And if I announce that I will build up and plant a certain nation or kingdom, making it strong and great, but then that nation turns to evil and refuses to obey me, I will not bless that nation as I had said I would. "Therefore, Jeremiah, go and warn all Judah and Jerusalem. Say to them, 'This is what the LORD says: I am*

> *planning disaster against you instead of good. So turn*
> *from your evil ways, each of you, and do what is right."*
> Jeremiah 18:1–11

In other words, as we've allowed our lives to be submitted to the Potter, the beautiful thing about it is that He does not throw us away. Wherever you are in business, you can always start with the right understanding, the right thought process, speaking the right things, and taking the right actions. The intention is that, wherever we are, we are still in the hands of the Potter, who is God, and He is constantly designing us, molding us, and making us. The work that He's begun in you and me, He shall perform it until the coming of Christ Jesus. So, be at peace in your business and be at peace in your personal life because when you've totally surrendered, you can expect to become a glorious vessel of honor in the workplace and where you reside.

During the formation of this book, I came across a video of a pastor preaching about a popular rap artist disrespecting Jesus in one of his songs. It illustrated for me that anyone can be used for the advancement of the Kingdom of God through Jesus. About three minutes into the recording, he says *"Jesus can't save you. Life starts when the church ends."* I was curious about how others were reacting to the lyrics, so I did a search on Google and YouTube and found responses from other pastors who were speaking about this song in their sermons. This search also led me to a video about another hip-hop artist stating that he'd been called into ministry by the Lord and he was producing a hip-hop Gospel CD. I went to the Scriptures in regard to all the types of people who were (and are) being used by God to move His agenda forward, even people like Judas. Without Judas, there still would have been a cross. Yet, there had to be a Judas, somebody had to play that role to betray Jesus in order for Him to go to the cross, as the story was being orchestrated by God. So, if that's the case, we all have a role to play, regardless of how many crazy records are produced or who debates over someone's lyrics. Regardless of why they said what they said, it caused people to stand on their convictions and begin to proclaim even louder than they had been before, really taking a stand for Jesus. Even a multimillionaire from the projects who makes a record in 2009 with lyrics that say *"Jesus can't save you. Life starts when the church ends,"* has a purpose in moving the agenda of Christ forward. At the end of the day, regardless of what's said about Jesus in 2009 or thousands of years ago when He was nailed to a cross and murdered, it is all a part of the agenda in God's plan. We know that even death could not hold Him. So, certainly those words on that American musician's record are nowhere near the magnitude of what took place on Calvary 2000 years ago. That ugly statement, in a three minute song, that took about three seconds to say is serving a purpose. We all have the ability to have an impact and, as we work harder to walk closer with God through Christ Jesus, we have an opportunity to continue to be perfected.

We are trusting that this will be a tremendous blessing for believers as well as nonbelievers, that all will come into a place where God can use them. Everything we do, we do unto God, realizing the work that has begun leads to our responsibility in surrendering freely unto the Lord.

CHAPTER 14

—⟨ℰℐℐ⟩—

Wisdom and Understanding

"Fear of the LORD is the beginning of wisdom. Knowledge of the Holy One results in understanding."

Proverbs 9:10

*T*here is a divine timing with God in the sense of being able to discern the times and make the appropriate decisions. It's really about making appropriate choices at the appropriate time and taking the appropriate actions at the appropriate time. From a personal standpoint, you must be in a position where you can make decisions based on all of the information that you have. The concept of wisdom is about knowledge and understanding because, as the proverb states, *"Wisdom is the principle thing, but in all thy getting get understanding"* (Proverbs 4:7). Understanding usually comes from experience or you can get it from the experience of someone else. When you think about the Word of God as the experience of the Creator of the universe laying out exactly how it is that we are to live, perform, and think, then we know that we can learn from whatever it is that He has laid out in His Word. Wisdom is contained in the Scriptures. It's contained in the stories that are in the Old

Testament as well as the New Testament. Wisdom is contained in the parables shared by Jesus with the disciples. So, we have an opportunity to recognize that we can certainly shorten our learning curve by leaning on the Word of God as our foundation and leaning on the Rock for our salvation, our actions, words, deeds, and work.

We have to make sure it's not just something that we're trying to get through on personal experience alone. A wise man will learn vicariously through the experiences of other people—meaning that you're not going to make the same mistakes that other people have made. You'll understand that it's not so much about right or wrong, but more about appropriate action. Are you taking the appropriate action at the appropriate time with the appropriate attitude for the appropriate reason? This concept of wisdom is something that sometimes comes with age, but that is not always the case. At the age of twelve, Christ was teaching in the synagogue. He had the scholars of the Scriptures, the Pharisees and the scribes, sitting at His feet as He shared with them the wisdom and the understanding of God. This doesn't mean you have to be eighty years old to gain wisdom. However, you do have to be in a position where you can understand that as you are using your eyes and your ears reading and digesting information and Scripture, which contains ageless wisdom, you make that part of you. Age is not a real issue here. What is at issue is where you are mentally as you read the Word of God, which will determine how much information you are able to glean. This is information that can come out of you as you encounter different scenarios and different circumstances in your life, making wisdom the principle thing. With all thy getting, get understanding.

One of the fundamentals of wisdom is that everyone appears to have an understanding as we look at the Scriptures. There was one key element that separated Solomon, who was considered the wisest man in the world. He understood and realized that, because he was already ordained to be king, he had all the wealth and resources, but his main concern was being sure that he was empowered and equipped with all the necessary tools to be successful in running his kingdom. How do I function? How do I navigate through the malaise and the transitions of the world to the interaction of people? Here is one of the key elements and key components: in order for you to be successful in your business, there's going to have to be wisdom.

What is wisdom? Some people equate knowledge to wisdom, but it's actually an understanding that's required to apply the knowledge that you've acquired. It's not necessarily leading from an educational standpoint, based on the amount of schooling that you've attained, because there are some individuals who have not had the rudiments of a higher level of education, but they've become some of the wisest individuals in the world. They learned, first of all, how to submit to the will and authority of God by having an intimate and personal re-lationship with Him. They understood that by allowing their natural ability to be enhanced with the supernatural wisdom of God, they could continually develop, cultivate, and move into a realm which would allow them to gain information and great favor in places that they otherwise never had the opportunity to go.

I just want to add this to your understanding in regard to wisdom because it gave Solomon the opportunity to stand before the people of God. You can find this in 1 Kings 4. The people understood that Solomon was actually a young child when he was given the throne by God, but *he* knew he could not operate in that realm without having the wisdom of God. So, as you're looking to understand how you take your business model wherever you go in the country, and the wis-dom that's required to do that, it has something to do with something that's outside of your ability to operate on a day-to-day basis. That means you're going to have to have the wisdom to interact and con-nect with the resources you need to facilitate your business. There's also going to be a supernatural wisdom required to understand how to cultivate and develop the right working relationships and to dis-cern those things that will be detrimental for the advancement of your agenda in promoting the advancement of the Kingdom of God.

So, it's very important to be able to identify and have the wis-dom to operate in the business realm. As we're looking at having a clear path before us, there's one particular Scripture found in 1 Kings where Solomon was faced with making a decision which was far beyond his ability. Some of you may be familiar with that story in 1 Kings, where there were two women who each had a child and one of the women lost her child to death. The woman who lost her child stole the living child, so the two women and the baby came before King Solomon, petitioning him to determine the rightful owner of the living child. Solomon decided that he would just split the child in half. Because the true mother of that child would rather lose her child than have him cut in half, Solomon was able to discern from her reaction, and through the wisdom of the Spirit of God, the judgment that should be made.

The whole crux of this chapter is to understand that without wisdom, without knowledge, the people of God perish. If you use the right wisdom in operating your business before you engage a plan, before you make agreements, and before you sign any type of paperwork, you need to do your due diligence. You need to make sure that what you're getting involved in is going to allow you to move forward in the realm in which you've been called.

The principle thing in this is understanding how to apply the knowledge you've attained. I just want to quickly make it applicable to the business realm. As you look at your business relationships right now, the people who you're involved with, what type of wisdom, what type of understanding do you have? How many people are you affecting? Are you doing what you're doing for selfish gain or are you doing something that is going to allow your place of business to flourish by using your opportunity to enhance the lives of the people who you've been assigned to? Ultimately, at the end of the day, our responsibility, as we understand *success on God's terms*, is that we understand the frailty of man. We understand that, even in His goodness and His mercy, we have a responsibility to uphold the wisdom of God, the principles of God and to act as change agents in the atmosphere and in the earth.

You must come to the understanding that your natural wisdom, your natural knowledge will never allow you to accomplish the things that you've been purposed to until you've submitted your mind, according to Proverbs 16:3, If you "commit your actions to the Lord... your plans will succeed." That's the first and foremost step in obtaining wisdom.

CHAPTER 15

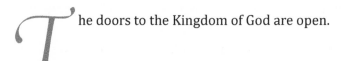

The Doors to the Kingdom of God Are Open

"Then he said to the crowd, 'If any of you wants to be my follower, you must turn from your selfish ways, take up your cross daily, and follow Me.'"

Luke 9:23

*T*he doors to the Kingdom of God are open.

"Then Jesus said, "Come to Me, all of you who are weary and carry heavy burdens, and I will give you rest. Take My yoke upon you. Let Me teach you, because I am humble and gentle, and you will find rest for your souls." Matthew 11:28–29

If you have not accepted Jesus the Christ as your Lord and Savior, we would be remiss if we did not take this opportunity at the conclusion of our dialogue to encourage you to do so.

The process of salvation is a simple one. The price has already been paid. You have been redeemed from the bondage of sin and eternal death through the death, burial, and resurrection of Jesus. All you have to do to be saved is accept and follow Jesus by believing in your heart that God raised him from the dead, confessing with your mouth that Jesus is Lord, and repenting from sin. To *repent* simply means *to turn away from sin*, but more importantly, *to turn toward God through Jesus*. He is the only way to the eternal life that is promised in the Bible. As a disciple of Jesus, just follow His leadership found in the Word of God. Scripture declares,

> *"For if you confess with your mouth that Jesus is Lord and believe in your heart that God raised him from the dead, you will be saved."* Romans 10:9

The Word also says, *"But to all who believed Him and accepted Him, He gave the right to become children of God."* John 1:12.

Find a local church to fellowship in and to grow into maturity as a twenty-first century disciple of Jesus.

Join us online at the http://FellowshipOfTheFlame.com and http://12StonesEd.org for social networking with Christians from across the globe and spiritual edification through multimedia Christian education and online training.

If you have already accepted Jesus as your Lord and Savior, our admonition is that you press deeper into your Father's business. Share this information with everyone in your center of influence; first by example as a living epistle and second by works and words. Remember, "the Kingdom of Heaven on earth" is possible because of the Spirit of God that abides in you while you walk the planet as an Ambassador for the Kingdom of Heaven. Selah!

CHAPTER **16**

—⌘—

Questions and Answers

"Don't give what is holy to unholy people. Don't give pearls to swine! They will trample the pearls, then turn and attack you." Keep on asking, and you will be given what you ask for. Keep on looking, and you will find. Keep on knocking, and the door will be opened. For everyone who asks, receives. Everyone who seeks, finds. And the door is opened to everyone who knocks. You parents—if your children ask for a loaf of bread, do you give them a stone instead? Or if they ask for a fish, do you give them a snake? Of course not! If you sinful people know how to give good gifts to your children, how much more will your heavenly Father give good gifts to those who ask him."

Matthew 7:6–11

Fear and Success

Question: What do you feel is one of the biggest fears that a person may have, for not reaching their full potential?

MR. GAMBRELL: Well, it's funny that you should talk about the word *fear*, because that word shows up many times as we study Scripture. And there are many times when Jesus is about to heal someone or give them what they're looking for and He asks them, He admonishes them, not to have fear—do not to be afraid. Many times when angels appear in Scripture, one of the first things out of their mouths—because people get so awestruck by their presence—is the encouragement not to be afraid, do not fear. So, we know that fear exists in all the things that we encounter at some level, and the idea is that you have to replace the thoughts of fear with the thoughts of faith. So, it's an equation for creation. As you think the thoughts of God and you speak the words of God, you have an opportunity to do the work of God in order to see that thing that He's already called forth for you. So all of the words that He has put forth in the universe through Jesus the Christ and the prophets will certainly come to fruition, they will not return void. He is looking for the people to send out into the vineyard, to help reap the harvest of souls. So, the idea is that you have to begin to focus on the things that you want and the things that are going to empower you versus focusing on that thing that is generating fear.

And your potential has been put in you for a reason. You have been gifted. There is something that you will be able to bring to the marketplace that no one else can bring to the marketplace. As you stand on the Word of God, it gives you the energy; you're empowered by the Holy Spirit. Your confidence is raised as you go from believing in God to having faith in God to knowing God. And it's a process. There's a difference between believing in God and having faith in God. There's a difference between having faith in God and knowing God. And that's the whole purpose of your walk with Christ Jesus. He wants to have a relationship with us. He wants us to know him intimately. And as we know him intimately, then it's almost like when a couple is together for fifty years, when the husband says the first part of the sentence and the wife completes the second part. And how, if you've ever been around a couple that has been married for fifty or sixty years and they're up in their years, they walk around communicating without even saying anything a lot of times. Because they know what the routine is, what the desire is, what the request is without words being spoken. So, God wants that kind of intimacy with you, but the only way that you can do that is by spending time with Him in his Word so that you can begin to be familiar with Him. Now, you know there are about 365 times in Scripture that the Word says do not fear, do not be afraid—it might be about 385 depending on the version that you're reading—but it's about one for every day of the year—don't be afraid, don't fear, don't have fear. There are so many stories and illustrations in Scripture that talk about fear and doubt. Currently, I'm studying the Book of Luke and I'll close with this.

In the first chapter of Luke, there are 80 verses in this chapter, and I've actually put a comment on my Facebook wall with regard to the fact that Zechariah, as well as Mary, were visited by angels. Gabriel was letting Zechariah know that John the Baptist was going to be born through Elizabeth, and the angel came to Mary to let her know the coming of Christ and her being the vessel that God had chosen. Zechariah encountered the angel and Zechariah was righteous before God. He was viewed righteous before God as well as Mary. But Zechariah doubted and he had fear and he was struck mute for nine months. Mary believed that it was possible for the Holy Spirit to impregnate her, even though she was a virgin. Mary believed it and we're still talking about Mary and her faith; we're still talking about Mary as the mother of Jesus. She's blessed all generations because of her belief. We don't really know about Zechariah that much even though he's the father of John the Baptist, but we know about Mary as the mother of the Son of God because of her stand, the stand that she took by just believing the Word of God. The Holy Spirit was active in both of those situations, but the Holy Spirit did not deal with Zechariah until John the Baptist was born, which means to me that his belief and his fear had to dissipate before the Holy Spirit could act in his life. So he doubted and he was struck mute for nine months. Mary and Elizabeth were visited by the Holy Spirit during their pregnancies. It was very interesting that they spent three months together as these babies were in their wombs. So fear incapacitates you, it's a mind-killer, and when you stand on the Word of God, you have an opportunity to do what you've been called to do and that's something that you have to recognize. But it's just an intimacy that you have to create with Jesus because we're standing on His strength. We're standing on His strength because of the frailty of our human composition; we have to stand on the spiritual strength of God through Jesus the Christ and the Comforter being the Holy Spirit.

Studying the Bible

Question: If we're to study the Bible, what is your suggestion? Do you suggest that we read the Bible from cover to cover, or pick out certain things? Usually, it's the interpretation that is the toughest part, especially in such a profound book.

MR. GAMBRELL: What was very helpful for me—and still is in my study of the Word of God, because it's an ongoing process—and one of the things that had a very profound impact on me, I actually purchased the Bible on CD and I listened to the entire Bible twice, through the CDs'. So listening to the audio was very significant for me. Also, as I first began my study of Scripture, one of my mentors told me there are thirty-one chapters in Proverbs and you should read a chapter each day, depending on what the date it is. Today is the 5th, so when I woke up this morning, I read Proverbs 5 and Psalm 5. A lot of times, as you are engaging the Scripture, it will lead you to other parts of the Bible.

Also, there are two Bibles that are very useful for me. There's the "Maxwell Leadership Bible" with notes and articles by John C. Maxwell, and then also the "Spirit Filled Life Student Bible, for Growing in the Power of the Word". These are both very popular Bibles and you can find them online or in a bookstore. The thing about these Bibles is that they have commentary in them to help you interpret the words. It's the New King James version, so it's not so much the old English. And then the last comment that I want to make is that the Amplified Bible is a very good tool as well, because the

Amplified Bible gives you synonyms, like a thesaurus, gives you the feel for certain words in the Scripture, so that you can understand the context of what's being said. When you do the cross-reference between the study Bibles and Bibles with commentary and the Amplified Bible, it will give you the flavor of what is being communicated in the Scripture. But the biggest thing is the yearning to spend time in the Word of God. It's almost like when you're dating or you're attracted to someone who you're looking to spend some time with— it's the same thing. You have to have that desire to spend time in the Word. And as you do that, you will find yourself flipping through the pages—that is one of the things that I do as well. If I am facing some adversity in my life, I'll just go to the Bible and open it and flip to a random page. I can't tell you the countless number of times that I've opened the Bible and there was the answer to what was happening, help for the challenge that I was having, or some word of inspiration, during a valley experience. Just go to the Bible, open it up, and start reading. That will help with your understanding.

Then you want to get you a good dictionary and concordance because it's back to the whole thought process. If you don't understand the words, it's hard to understand what's being said, the context of what's being said. That's the same as reading any kind of book. Most of the time when reading, people skip over words that they don't know or have the definition for and it diminishes their understanding of what they are reading. Mr. Rogers do you have any additional commentary?

MR. ROGERS: Yes, I definitely want to add something to it. Folks, as we're talking about *success on God's terms*, what we're really speaking of is developing the proper characteristics of God. And by developing the proper characteristics of God, then there's going to be a natural law of attraction and you're going to be able to attract those things that are conducive to you emulating and representing your power source: God. He says, *"Let us create man and make man in our own likeness and image."* So we've been pre-programmed to replicate the Creator. What happens is that we missed a line because of misinformation or improper thought processes, so our characteristics diminish. We all have been created to have proper talent, but now this process of committing our thoughts and our works unto the Lord gives us the right characteristics, the right attributes, which allow us to have total dominion and to replicate in the marketplace. That's why it's very important to infuse yourself with the proper thoughts, and proper thoughts will then align into proper actions. Proper actions will then lend themselves to proper influence. And proper influence will allow us to have total reign and total control over what we've been assigned to and given stewardship over.

The influence is key, because we've been in situations where either we've experienced it ourselves as the person who was doing it, or we've watched it happen, where you have a man of God who everyone knows is a man of God—he might be a pastor or someone else in the community who's just outstanding; and you can be cutting up using all kinds of crazy language, but when that person comes into your presence, you make an adjustment. That's called *influence.* That means that that person is representing something that is affecting the way that you interact and behave with him. You might be using profanity, telling off-color jokes or whatever, but when that person comes into your presence, the profanity stops and you straighten up with regard to the content of your dialogue and your language. That's the type of impact that we want to have as business owners; that's the type of impact that we want to have as parents; that's the type of impact that we want to have in our communities.

We want to be able to go into a situation and everybody adjusts and lines up with our agenda, because our agenda is God's agenda with regard to establishing the Kingdom of Heaven on earth. People will begin to line up with that, based on the influence that we have. And anything that is out of divine order will flee from God's plan.

The Word does not say go ahead and hit the devil upside the head and he will flee. Scripture says resist the devil and he will flee. That means to just resist in the presence, and in the presence things that are out of divine order will correct themselves because the power and the Word of God are the strongest.

The power of God and the Word of God are the strongest things in the earthly realm. But we have to represent that power and get it out of the Word. Get it out of that book, allow it to live in us, and then we become the vessels; we carry the Word around wherever we go. You could be at a Little League game or a board meeting. It really doesn't matter. It's just that power of God, that anointing, resting in you and everyone adjusts accordingly.

He's given us the perfect prescription for all the ills of the world, the ailments of the world and society, whether they're spiritual, mental, emotional, physical, or financial. So, we have to be intimate with that, and the more intimate with Him that we become, the more confident we become. Then we begin to reap the rewards that He's laid up for us and the treasures not only pertaining to money, but to things like peace and joy—peace of mind. I'm not talking about happiness, but I'm talking about peace and joy. There's a difference—People are pursuing happiness and it's a very elusive thing because happiness is based on something that's happened outside of you. Peace and joy come from inside.

Recognizing the Voice of God

Question: If we're growing in our faith walk, constantly on a daily basis, how can we condition ourselves mentally and spiritually as far as our salvation is concerned, so that we can readily recognize God's voice when He's calling us? So that there's no feeling of uncertainty or doubt; is that God's voice or is it not? How can we condition ourselves? What steps can we take so that we can know without a shadow of a doubt that we're doing what God wants us to do on a daily basis?

MR. GAMBRELL: When a baby is born, they're pretty much born blind; they can't see past a couple of inches beyond their face. One of the reasons, in my mind, that that is the case is that their mind is fresh; they've just been born and if they were able to see everything around them, it would really bombard their senses. It would bombard their brains. So they're able to see just far enough to recognize, in a fuzzy way, the contours of their mother's face, and their hearing is extra sensitive—children jump at loud noise, even into their toddler years. But one of the things that they do know, beyond a shadow of a doubt, even before coming out of the womb, because of the sound and vibrations that take place during that nine-months of pregnancy, they know the voice of their parents. For you to know the voice of God, you need to be in a relationship with God in an intimate way, so that when He speaks outside of the Scripture, you will know whether that Word is coming from God or the person speaking. In order to work out the situation and not allow external things or negative reports to sway you, you have to be grounded in the good report of the Gospel. You have to be grounded in the Good News. And if you're grounded in the Good News and somebody says something contrary to it, it doesn't faze you because you know that that negativity is contrary to the Word of God. And you know anything contrary to the Word of God is about failure and that is one thing that God cannot do, fail.

If you start listening to the voices of other people, especially people who do not line up with the Word of God, then you will get what those individuals are projecting. There's never a recession in God's economy. God has all the money. God has all the resources and all the witty ideas. If you're lined up with that, it doesn't matter what the so—called experts are saying. It doesn't even matter what I'm saying, because if I'm saying something that's contrary to the Word of God, and you know the Word of God, you will know what contradicts it. It's the same thing when people are mislead by pastors and evangelists—the reason that they're able to be misled is that they don't know the Word for themselves.

You need to work out daily in the Word of God, so that that Word gets inside of your heart. And then, anything that's not lining up with that Word will be apparent, whether it has to do with business, personal relationships or anything else. That's the whole idea of this particular project and the movement that we're creating with this book. It's not about just being successful, because Joshua 1:8 talks about *good* success, not just success. There are a bunch of ways that we can be successful by the world's standards, but the good success that God talks about is captured throughout His Word in the New and the Old Testaments.

This is what you do. You have to know for yourself. And anything coming against that, whether it is coming from a professor or your classmates or your Pastor, then it shouldn't faze you because you know the ultimate authority is the Word of God and He's already proclaimed the victory for you.

Mr. Rogers did you want to add anything?

MR. ROGERS: And simply understanding that is just like simply digesting the Word. It goes back to the very beginning, where we started. When you know the Word of God, you're able to replace negative thoughts with God's thoughts. The Apostle Paul would address that in 2 Corinthians, chapter 10, where the Word says that our warfare is not carnal, but is mighty by pulling down strongholds and bringing every thought into the obedience of Christ. In other words, because you have the Word of God in you, any time you hear something contrary to the Word of God, then you're automatically able to replace that with the truth, because you know His truth.

And truth is a person, and you've met the truth in the person of Christ Jesus. So those who know Him and respond to His voice—you will not follow the voice of a stranger. That's the importance of making sure that you're on a day-to-day basis with the Word of God. Not just reading the Word but ingesting it, so that it becomes a part of your being. Then you are able to ward off the negative voices, you're able to shield your ears, and you're able to hide the Word in your heart. As David said, you hide the Word in your heart, so that you may not sin against the Lord thy God and walk in the statutes and the way that He's purposed.

And I'm excited to know that, no matter what the circumstance, there's always been a precedent that God has established and this is it: He's never left His people without His presence, without His power, or without His provision. Everything is sustained by God. We're told in the Word that man cannot live by bread alone, but by every word that proceeds out of the mouth of God. Physically, Elijah was in a place where it was barren, where it was destitute, where it was dry. Under those circumstances, it was totally unnatural for a raven to feed anyone because ravens are scavengers and they consume things and they keep them and they hoard things for themselves, but God used these ravens to care for Elijah. Because you understand that and know the power and the agreement that was established, before you and I had an opportunity to audition, and because we received the manifold grace of God in Christ Jesus, then we're now privileged to walk in the office we've been called to.

The Condition of Your Heart

Question: When Mr. Rogers was speaking about the condition of your heart, he was saying if your heart's not where it needs to be then your goals and aspirations will not come to fruition? Is that what you were saying?

MR. ROGERS: Yes, everything has to be properly lined up. As we started out this series, Proverbs 16:3 is a good example: as we commit our thoughts unto the Lord, then He will establish our work. The peace and calm comes from knowing, because you now have the heart of God according to Jeremiah 3:15, that your purpose is to feed his people with knowledge and understanding. That's our mandate, that's our responsibility, so we will not violate the essence or the character of God. We achieve this by simply having His heart, because His thoughts toward us are good and not evil. You understand that God says in the last days, *"I will write my word upon the fleshly parts of your heart, that no man need to teach you or guide you."*

It's already innate in us and our responsibility is simply to feed ourselves with the Word of God, so that it will stir up what's already in us. In that way, we can respond properly because in the very beginning, God said, *"Let us make man and create man in our likeness and our image."* And we have to position ourselves in a place where our dominant thought is the Spirit of God, which is the Heart of God, this allows us to move and walk in a manifestation of God, which, in turn, allows us to see the manifestation of the Kingdom of Heaven on earth. We're ambassadors of the Kingdom of Heaven and that's our natural-born right, because we were reborn and regenerated into the right family. Because we've been regenerated, we have the right heart and the willingness to be obedient to the Word of God, so we operate in that supernatural realm.

Question from Mr. Gambrell: I have a question for Mr. Rogers. I just had a thought about this concept of when you mentioned the word *regeneration*, thinking about the rebirth—well, let me put it like this—as human beings, we are triune beings, and we have a physical birth and then we have this conscious decision that we have to make in order to accept Christ from a thought-process standpoint. How is that correlated to the concept of transformation or regeneration, given that we are triune beings? What hit me as you were talking is that when we make our mental decision to follow Christ, then would you consider it truth that He completes the process of regeneration to give us that full spiritual birth, allowing us to go through three stages of being born; a physical birth, a soul rebirth, and then a final spiritual regeneration? What are your thoughts on that?

MR. ROGERS: Yes, that's absolutely the case and that's the importance of understanding our responsibility to share the Gospel. Because that allows us to have our rights and privileges restored because our hearts have been regenerated. And, according to the Word of God, without the shedding of blood, there will be no remission of sin. The power behind that regeneration, that new birth, the new heart that we receive, simply means that we're back to the initial state, the original plan that God had for us. And that gives us the ability to walk in our spiritual authority and to overcome all natural obstacles and dilemmas that we may face, because we are able to excel above those obstacles. It's all a matter of the heart.

Out of the mouth confession is made, but it's based on what's coming out of our hearts. That's what the dual formula represents, according to Romans chapter 10: we come into the saving knowledge of Christ Jesus, if we confess with our mouths *and* believe in our hearts that God raised Jesus from the dead; then we will be saved. So, everything we have is a matter of heart. The understanding is simply this, when God gets our heart, then our minds will belong to Him as well.

For so long we've tried to do it the opposite way around. We have tried to let Him have our minds, but then our hearts are in conflict. So, it's heart first and then the mind. Then we're able to operate and move. Then, according to Matthew 6:33, *"seek ye first the kingdom of God and his righteousness and all these things* [that the heathens seek after] *will be added unto you."* And that's every realm of success, from a material standpoint, from an emotional standpoint, from a psychological standpoint—it was completed in the price paid by Christ Jesus.

MR. GAMBRELL: So the full understanding is that you have a physical birth, you have a soul birth, and you also have a spiritual birth.

MR. ROGERS: Absolutely.

MR. GAMBRELL: Then is this why—I was just reading this and making a connection—in the Book of Matthew, chapter 13, verse 15—I'll just read the whole verse, *"For this people's heart has become calloused, they hardly hear with their ears, they close their eyes, otherwise they might see with their eyes, hear with their ears, understand with their heart, and turn and I will heal them."* There's nothing that we can do, it's just a work that God has to complete in us as it relates to the full maturity from a spiritual standpoint. We have to turn and submit and give it over to Him and repent in order for Him to complete the work that He started in us since Adam. Would you say that might be a nice wrap-up?

MR. ROGERS: That is absolutely it. He's the one who has to complete the process, but the remedy, the solution has been made available to each and every one of us, as we continually proclaim and point people to the only thing that's going to allow that regeneration to take place, and that's what our responsibility is. To point them to the cross of Jesus the Christ.

Obedience Is Better than Sacrifice

Question: How do you think obedience relates to sacrifice in the sense of obedience being better than sacrifice? What exactly does that mean?

MR. GAMBRELL: In the Old Testament, you were to take sacrifices to the altar and only the high priest could go in to the presence of God. He had to sanctify himself and go through a whole purification process. People would bring sacrifices to the temple to atone for their sins, which was really a parallel to the price that Jesus had to pay for the sin of the world, past, present, and future. He had to experience the death of the cross, so that is why Jesus is called the Lamb—He was the sacrificial Lamb of God.

People would bring animals to the priests for sacrifice because the people had been disobedient. That particular verse of Scripture is saying that it is better to obey first than to sacrifice later, after being disobedient, bringing your sacrifices to the altar to atone for your sins. We often fall short of where we're supposed to be and we end up having to make sacrifices, but it is better to obey than to require a sacrifice. It's better to be righteous than unrighteous and that's really what that verse is saying. This is especially true when you have the

Word, you've heard the Word, you're aware of the Word, and you go against it, it's better to obey than have to repent. Mr. Rogers', do you have anything you would like to add?

MR. ROGERS: We have to understand sacrifice. Saul was given a commandment to obey and God had given him specific instructions and he did partially what God had instructed him to do. Sometimes, when we find ourselves doing partially what God instructs and experience that shortcoming then that requires sacrifice. Had Saul been obedient to everything that God had instructed him to do, then the Kingdom and everything that God had promised him would have been fulfilled. But Saul chose to be more concerned about pleasing the people than about pleasing God. That's really what we're talking about when we talk about being obedient to God and His plan. It's better to obey God. You will never be able to please man and that's pretty much the crux of what true obedience requires.

First, we must have total submission to God, and any time we find our lives in conflict with people, if it's not a conflict with God and being obedient in bringing honor and glory to Him, He will make the adjustments and protect, guide, and direct us when we come into conflict with man. If Saul had been obedient to God, the kingdom would never have been taken from him. Because of his disobedience, because he chose not to follow God's Word exactly, he found himself losing the kingdom.

We put ourselves in those same situations time and time again. Just as C. Thomas said, we know what to do, we just choose not to obey in its entirety and then we end up making a sacrifice, which is only for a short period of time. Ultimately, out of repentance, we turn away from that thing and we're willing to obey. Then, out of our obedience, we can expect the true manifestation of every promise that was intended for us.

Do Not Despise Small Beginnings

Question: When you were talking about "do not despise small beginnings," is that coming from Zechariah 4:10 or is there another part of the Bible you're referencing?

MR. ROGERS: That is one of the places where it's found and, when you think about what you are, you started out with small beginnings, as an egg and a sperm. So, never despise small beginnings, never despise where you are and whatever your business endeavor is, because as you nurture those things properly and provide the proper nutrition, then you will reap a harvest because you're willing to water the seed you have been instructed to plant. God is a God of multiplication. As we stated from the very beginning, He only creates to make it perpetual. So, never despise small beginnings.

Closing Prayer

Father God, we come humbly before You, saying thank You for Your continued grace and Your mercy, for it's because of You that we've been designed and created to do everything that we do. Our desire and continual prayer is for individuals hearts to receive this message of *Success on God's Terms* and we pray that it would return to You one hundred fold, that Your name would be blessed and all glory would go to Your name. Bless each and every reader's family right now, whatever the situation is, emotionally, physically, financially, we pray because of the Word that was said, that it would transform their entire perspective of who You are—bring them closer into a relationship with You and help them surrender their will to Yours. We realize and we say thank You—it's all because of Your power and Your Spirit that we're able to do anything. We pray that You would never withdraw Your Spirit from us, that You would continually give us strength, that You would meet every need of all who read this book. More importantly, we pray that those individuals will always act on the ideas and talents that You have given them. That they will replicate and bring You a one-hundred fold harvest, according to Your Word. We say thank you. We ask these blessings in Your Son Jesus' name. Amen. Selah!

PART 4

Bonus Limited Deluxe Edition Content

Success on God's Terms: 31 Modes of a Virtuous Woman

———— ◦◦◦ ————

By Shamira Pongnon-Howie

This bonus chapter is a glimpse into the *31 Modes of a Virtuous Woman* with focus on the single woman. *31 Modes of a Virtuous Woman* is about living your life according to God's principles.

*T*he Word of God says in Genesis 2:18, the Lord God said that it was *"not good"* for man to be alone. Note this is the *only* time during the story of creation that God said *anything* was "not good." In Proverbs 18:22 NKJV, it says: *"He who finds a wife finds with a good thing and obtains favor from the LORD."* Note that finding a wife is a good thing and he receives God's favor for doing so.

So, let's examine what should be happening while the man is seeking. While he is seeking and preparing to choose and love, you should be going into Esther mode, Hannah mode, Ruth mode, Proverbs 31 woman mode, Abigail mode, Rachel mode, etc. There are numerous examples and characteristics of women in the Bible that provide a template or guide as to steps you can take to be the woman God has called you to be, and that is a good thing.

Esther mode is about preparation, wise counsel, and courage. Queen Esther was the wife of King Xerxes. Before she became the

Queen, she was prepared to be chosen. After Queen Vashti disrespected the King, he began a search for a new Queen. He was seeking and Esther was preparing. She prepared for twelve months prior to her first meeting with the King. Esther was working on herself while the King was seeking. Although many women desire to be married, many have an "as-is" mentality. The reality is if we take an honest look at ourselves there are things that we may want to change or improve in ourselves. Those things that we desire to change within ourselves are those things that will make us more attractive to him that is seeking. If you think or feel that "as-is" you are where you need to be, then you can stop reading here. However, if you agree that there are areas where you would like to enhance, then let Esther be an example. We must spend time in preparation for the things we desire.

In Esther's example, it discusses beauty treatments repeated over the course of two six-month periods. We know that beauty has both inner and outer aspects. We can use her timeline as a guide to work on our beauty. You know what things about you make you "ugly" or what characteristics you possess that you should take time to further cultivate and enhance. Take some time to yourself to do a self-inventory, twelve months to go from "as-is" to "under construction" to "renovated."

Esther also had wise counsel to guide her along her journey. Change is a journey. Whose counsel are you following? The key term here is *wise*. The Bible doesn't say Esther sat around talking with her girlfriends who were in the same predicament that she was in or who were bitter about things from the past. Exercise discernment when you accept counsel from someone. It should be someone who puts God first and has your best interests at heart. Believe it or not, sometimes those closest to you do not have your best interests at heart. Ask God to give you discernment in this area. When she was faced with a difficult situation, Esther sought out God's direction as well as wise counsel from others.

Esther is also an example of courage. She had the courage to do the right thing, which is not always the popular thing. In her case, she had to go before the King without being sent for, which was against the law. She later had to reveal her heritage. She did these things to take a stand for her people through God and what was right. Do we have this same courage today? Are we willing to take a stand for God and what is right? Are we willing to say no to premarital sex (fornication) because, although it is accepted by society, it goes against God's Word? How courageous are you? Esther was courageous up to the possibility of death—Esther 4:16. Examine your lifestyle and see how it lines up with the Word of God. The more you align your life with God's Word, the more successful you will be.

The story of Esther gives us a model to follow with regard to dealing with difficult situations. In everything, we must calculate the cost and set priorities, after which we must prepare ourselves. Last of all, we have to determine which course of action we will take and then, just as Esther did, we have to move ahead boldly. Remember this model the next time you face a difficult situation.

In Esther mode, we prepare, seek wise counsel, and exercise courage to stand for what is right. Remember to trust God and prepare to be surprised by the ways He demonstrates His trustworthiness.

A Proverbs 31 Woman is you, me, and all obedient women of God. A Proverbs 31 woman knows that God is her head and source of strength. Therefore, she is able to do all things, all great things through Jesus Christ whom she serves. She cooks, cleans, is an excellent mother, educated, an advocate, philanthropist, she's creative, a role model, an achiever, a soul mate to her husband, and a matriarch to her family. She leads by example and possesses the skills of leadership and discernment, yet exercises humility, all through Jesus.

The Proverbs 31 woman is the bride of the Lord; therefore, she is made perfect in His sight through the sacrifices of Jesus. She is a woman of excellence and her relationship with God sets her apart from all the other women in the land. She knows her value, and carries herself with the air of royalty because she knows she is the wife of the Almighty King! She is beautiful, not only on the outside but on the inside because she has a heart for God and she knows that her body is a temple—therefore, she takes excellent care of it!

She is loyal because she learned all of her lessons of faithfulness through Christ Jesus. The Proverbs 31 Woman is who she is because she knows her role and her place in the divine order of God and she allows her Lord to guide her footsteps!

To be continued. . .

For more on the *31 Modes of a Virtuous Woman* visit http://31Modes.com and follow Sister Shamira Pongnon-Howie on Twitter at: http://twitter.com/31modes

Success on God's Terms: The Economic Story of the Hunter and the Lion

By Dr. Craig Bythewood

I would like to share 1 Samuel 22:2 with you, but before I actually provide the Scripture, let me just remind you that when discussing the text, it's very important that we think about what's actually going on, what preceded this particular text, so that if we think about the pre-text and think about the post-text, we can put the Scripture in context. So, what's going on right now is that David is fleeing persecution from Saul, who has already been told that David will be the king and, Saul being the king at that moment, wants to kill him. He sends out individuals to kill David. David, being aware of that, decides he wants to gather several individuals to fight with him as an army. At this point, in 1 Samuel 22:2, he is gathering individuals to fight with him, and it reads,

> *"And everyone that was in distress, and everyone that was in debt, and everyone that was discontented gathered themselves unto him and he became a captain over them."*
> 1 Samuel 22:2

Now, it's a very simple Scripture. Basically, what David is doing is very logically assuming that those individuals who are in distress or are discontented or in debt and feel they have nothing to lose will be the perfect soldiers. What I pulled out of this Scripture is that God has a perception that we seem to have forgotten here in America and that is that God uses the word *stress*, the word *discontented* and the word *debt* as synonyms. He feels that our being in debt is just as bad as being distressed and just as bad as us being discontented.

This week, I was driving in my car and I heard a commercial that said, *"You don't want to have income because income is going to force you to pay taxes to the government, but call our firm and we'll teach you how to use corporate debt so that you can use debt instead of income."* Now, how ridiculous is it for a company to say to us, rather than make money, it's better for us to be indebted so that we can get the things done that we need to do.

So, before I really get into my message, I just wanted to throw out a couple of numbers to put this in perspective. There is a calculation that we do every year called the *Savings Rate*. The Savings Rate is a very simple calculation, a fraction that puts income in the denominator, (income is all the money that you and I make). In the numerator, it has savings, so *savings divided by income*. The guesstimation of savings is simply *that amount of money that we do not spend*, whether you put it in a retirement plan, a savings account, even if you put it at home in a mattress. If you do not spend it, it's in the numerator. All the money we make, goes in the denominator. Well, in the 1980s, the average savings rate was 9%. So, that means for every dollar that we made, we put away 9 cents. Hear me when I tell you that in this decade the savings rate has been as low as -2%. So, we've gone from 9% to -2%. By me saying negative, some of that calculation means we're spending more than we're making, but in today's society, we're trying to think of that as a good thing. We're trying to think of it as being able to have leverage, being able to purchase things that we may not be able to afford, but the Word of God says stress, discontent, and debt are synonymous.

The Hunter and the Lion African Proverb

There's an African proverb that reads, "*A little boy asked his father 'Why does the lion always die at the end of the story?' And the father said, 'It will always be that way until the lion begins to write the story.'*" But this is an African proverb, so I like to use it as an analogy, for the institutions and the organizations that run our society are like hunters and you and I as consumers are like lions. What ends up happening is that rules are set up along the way and we literally end up doing exactly what these institutions want us to do. They end up dying an economic death at the end of all of our stories because we think of it in terms of what we should and could do as opposed to looking at the hunter and what he's trying to get us to do. I have a million examples that I could give to you to represent what I call *hunter lionism*, but let me use just one, the banking industry.

The Banking Industry

A bank is an organization that takes deposits, they pay interest on those deposits, turn around and makes loans, and then charge interest on the loans. The difference between the interest rates charged on the loans versus the interest rates paid on those deposits represents their profits. Now, you don't have to answer this, I just want you to think about it. How many of us would still go to work if our jobs stopped paying us? If our jobs simply said to us, "I'm sorry, I'm no longer going to be able to pay you," would you continue to go? None of us would do that. Do you understand the way the model works? We give our time, our energy, our effort, and in turn they compensate us. I find it very interesting that we don't look at banks the same way.

The model of the bank that I just explained says that we give them the deposits and we're supposed to be paid interest, but you and I don't get paid interest. Why do you and I not get paid interest? Because you and I focus on the verb, not the noun; focus on the verb not the noun because you and I keep our money in checking accounts. Think about the first time you signed up for direct deposit, think about the form: name, address, Social Security number. What comes next? Checking account number. I've never been to the bank with any of you, but why am I so sure that when you go to the bank, whatever your transaction is, the first thing they say is, "Is that going into checking?" The bank has set it up so that you and I are encouraged to put our money in checking accounts, to *keep* our money in checking accounts. If we keep our money in checking, we don't get paid. The hunter has moved.

Now, I know what you're thinking. Some of you are thinking, well, what should I do with it? How should I arrange it? It's very important, if you're going to get anything out of this, don't focus on what you should do, but focus on the way the hunter is writing our story. Once we're doing what we should do and focus on the facts, then you and I are very comfortable with getting paid from our job, but you and I are not getting paid by banks because we keep our money in checking accounts.

Water on the Table

I was explaining this to an audience about eight years ago in Sarasota, Florida, and I was getting a little bit of venom from the audience. They were defending checking accounts as I was trying to make this point. To reinforce this point, I went and gathered one of those water dispensers and a pitcher of water that was in a hotel room and I put it in the middle of the table. Then, I said, "Let's pretend that this pitcher of water represents our checking account." I took a glass of water and said, "Let's pretend this represents our salary." Then I took an empty glass and said, "Let's pretend this represents our bills." So, pitcher of water—checking account; glass of water—salary; and empty glass—bills. So, I asked the group, "How many times do we get paid in a year?" They said twenty-six. Literally, twenty-six times I took the salary glass and poured it into the checking account pitcher, took the checking account pitcher and poured it into the bills glass; took the salary and poured it into the checking account; took the checking account and poured it into bills; took the glass of water and poured it into the pitcher; took the pitcher and poured it into the empty glass. By the time I had done that twenty-six times, there was water all over the table. I asked the group, "Why is there water on the table?" Someone said, "Because you're using the same container to pour water in as you are to pour water out," and I said, "Exactly." Isn't that what we do with our checking accounts?

We're constantly pouring money in and pouring money out at the same time. Let me explain to you what you and I are leaving on the table.

The average annual amount collected by banks every year, the average annual amount collected by banks on an annual basis from bounced check fees is in excess of $6 billion! You and I are not getting paid because we keep our money in checking accounts and now they're collecting a cool $6 billion a year because you and I are using the same account to pour money in as we are to pour money out. Now, recently I found out that the actual amount is $20 billion. The difference between $6 billion and $20 billion represents overdraft fees. I want you to think about something because oftentimes when I present this information, people will raise their hands and say, "Well, I don't have to worry about bounced check fees because I have overdraft protection." I used to have a truck and every time I would put it in reverse, it would make a noise—beep, beep, beep, beep—and alert me that I was moving backward, but because I had that alert, I oftentimes wouldn't actually look back. There was no reason for me to look back because I knew the truck would beep if there was anything behind me. That became kind of dangerous because sometimes I would drive my wife's car and put her car in reverse and I would forget to look back because I was so used to the protection that the beep gave me. Guess what? Overdraft protection is the same thing—it's a beep and because you know you have overdraft protection, you don't look behind you. So, we lose $14 billion a year because of overdraft protection. It should become clear at this point that the hunter does a good job of reflecting situations in a way where we get trapped, and we die an economic death at the end of the story.

The First Hit for Free

Now, please hear me—this is not about banks. This is about the way organizations present themselves. Let me ask you an unrelated question that you don't have to answer. What is the number one trick that a drug dealer uses to get a new customer? Answer: giving the customer the first hit for free. It's brilliant! Give them the first hit for free and they'll become so accustomed to it, so used to it, so addicted to it, that then they will pay whatever amount the dealer asks. Are you aware of the fact that when online banking first came out it was free? Now it isn't. Now, I do recognize that some institutions do not charge for online banking, but my point is that there was no such thing as an online banking charge when the service first came out. Are you aware that ATM cards, when they first came out, were free? They're not free now. In fact, the average ATM cost per transaction per card per person is $2.57. Did you know that when debit cards came out they were free? Some of you are thinking, "Okay, I was with him until he said debit card," since there are fees associated with debit cards, but let me give you two counterexamples.

About five years ago, I received a document from my credit union that said I owed a $6 charge. I wasn't sure what the charge was, so I called my credit union and they said to me, "That's your annual fee for your debit card." I explained to the young lady that I did not have a debit card and she said to me, "Everyone has a debit card." Interesting response. In order for me to prove that I'd never been issued a debit card, I had to get an authorized affidavit just to show that I'd never been issued one, for them to remove that small $6 charge. So, my first counterexample is that when debit cards first came out, they were free. Now, they're charging an annual fee.

Second counterexample: In 2003, a law was passed. It has not gone into effect yet. I'm pretty sure that it will not until the economy begins to rebound, but this particular law allowed them, the banking industry, to put into effect a slight fee that every time you use your debit card, you will be charged a fee.

With those three examples I just gave you, what is the difference between what drug dealers do and what banks do? The answer is: nothing, it's exactly the same. Now, it would be unfair for me to tell you that I do not have an ATM card and I do not have a debit card and not tell you why. So, let me address the second one by asking this question: in order for us to use the debit cards that everyone has, where do we have to put our money? In a checking account. Boy, the hunter is smooth! By forcing us to use debit cards, by making debit cards the next best thing since sliced bread, we're all letting the bank write our story for us because (a) we're not getting paid interest, (b) we're giving them a cool $20 billion a year in bounced check and overdraft fees, and (c) because of using debit cards, we don't even have an opportunity to keep our money anywhere, but in our checking account.

Let me tell you why I don't have an ATM card. Am I the only one who has ever been on a diet for some short-term reason? Well, if you were on a diet, would you take your favorite high calorie, high fat food and put it everywhere around you? Suppose your food is Krispy Kreme donuts. Would you put a box of donuts on your coffee table? A box of donuts in your car? A box of donuts on your desk at work? Would you put a box of donuts in your bedroom? A box of donuts in the bathroom? A box of donuts everywhere you go, so that as you continue to walk through the day you could see the box? Of course not! Why not? Because it's temptation! It's too easy for you to eat a donut if it's right there. Well, guess what? I am on a financial diet. ATMs are everywhere. It's very difficult for me to maintain a budget if I know all I have to do is just swipe a card and get some money anywhere I am at any point in time.

Write Your Own Economic Story

Now, I understand, it's unfair of us to give you all of these negative scenarios of these hunter ways that these banks use on us and not provide you with a way to get out of it. So, let me give you a brief synopsis of how we can write our own economic story to address issues like this. Before doing that, let me say one more time: this is so not about banks. This is about understanding the way the game is played and about understanding how things are set up so that we can make the best decisions. Please let me give you an off-the-wall example.

I have five daughters from the ages of five to eleven. If I go to my daughters and I say to my daughters, "Don't have sex," that's not going to work. In fact, I can think of at least one of them who will do it just because I told her not to. But, instead of giving them a rule or a strategy, I teach them how the game works. I explain to them what men are thinking and what the little boy is going to say If he says, "Baby, if you love me, you would," that means this, and if he takes you to McDonald's, he's going to have this expectation. If I let them understand the way the hunter in this particular paradigm thinks, I've now increased the chances that they'll make better decisions. That's exactly what I'm attempting to do through this dialogue. I'm exposing to you the way the organization thinks, the way the hunter thinks, so you're in a better position to make the right decisions.

Again, it's not about banks. It's about understanding the organizational perspective. Here's what I do: I take the money that I make and I direct-deposit it into some interest-bearing account. Sometimes when I present this material, there's frustration because people want to know exactly what interest-bearing account to put it in, and I don't give you that information, on purpose. Who knows, you may find an interest-bearing account that's better than anything I might I suggest. It's not about where you put the money, it's about you getting paid. Take this analogy: let's say you have a twenty-five-year-old child who is living in your house. You really wouldn't care where they worked, you just want them to work. You just want them to get paid. That's how I feel about this particular step. It doesn't matter where you put the money; it just matters that you get paid.

If I put my money into a direct-deposit account, an interest-bearing account, and then I do the same thing everyone else does, I make purchases. Now, most of the purchases that I make, I do so on a product that is called a charge card. What is a charge card? A charge card is just like a credit card, except you have to pay it off every thirty days. The only charge card that exists in America right now is American Express. I told you about the charge card before I mentioned the company American Express because American Express has many products, including credit cards. So, the two reasons why I use an American Express charge card...

The first reason I use an American Express charge card is discipline. If I know that I'm going to be putting something on this card, then I know I have to pay it off in thirty days. I'm not going to put anything on there, unless I have the money. The second reason I use American Express is that charge cards can make more purchases because I have a very active and aggressive program called membership rewards. The way it works is that for every dollar that I spend, I get a certain number of points and these points can be traded for different things. I started doing this when I was in graduate school in 1989. For three years, I used my American Express for my own purchases, which were groceries and gas. After three years, I took my points and I traded them in for a camcorder. I actually used that camcorder for about twelve years before the technology changed. I went to Howard University for undergraduate studies. Every single year, I go to Howard University's homecoming for free by trading in my points. My brother and my sister graduated from college the same weekend in Connecticut. I got two plane tickets and rented a car—free, just traded in my points. My best friend got married in Houston several years ago. I got two plane tickets, hotel, and rental car—free. I traded in my points. I'm very aggressive about using the American Express because, by doing so, it puts me in the position where I know I'm only going to put something on there that I can afford. Also, it gives me the ability to get different things. About five or six years ago, I began to, instead of traveling, trying to get different products. I got a VCR/DVD combo free—traded in my points. One year I got a five-in-one Hewlett-Packard printer, scanner, photo, copy machine free—just traded in my points.

I'd like to share this quick story: One of my children, at the time she was five, was sick when the UPS man delivered the printer. The question to me was, "Oh, Daddy, we bought a new printer?" I said, "No, actually, I got it for free." So, this five year old wanted to know, "How did you get it for free?" So, I got out a piece of paper and I explained to her exactly what I've explained to you. She said to me, "Oh, that's why you're always pulling out that gold card every time we go somewhere." A few months later, we were at the mall. I pulled out the card and I heard her whispering to her sisters, "Daddy's using that card so we can get free stuff." I'm buying the same things everybody else is buying, but I'm trying aggressively to write my own economic story.

Now, let's continue this analysis. For thirty days, what I do is purchase things. I'm very aggressive about using American Express—my second mortgage, American Express; cable bill, American Express; my cell phone bill, American Express. Wherever they allow me to use American Express, I do it. Now, at the end of the month, American Express sends me a bill. The bill says you owe us in thirty days. What that means is for sixty days, my money is sitting in an account earning interest. Everybody else's money is sitting in their checking account until they swipe it. The money's gone. I'm doing what everyone else is doing, I'm buying the same things that everyone else is buying, but I'm finding a way to look at what everyone else is doing—to look at the way the hunter is trying to set me up, to find a way to get compensated, and then putting myself in a position where I can write my own economic story. I have to say this again: this is so not about banks. This is about looking at what institutions are trying to get us to do and finding a way to write our own economic story.

The Credit Card Scripture

Now, I've been speaking for way too long without mentioning the mighty and powerful Word of God, so let me go back to it by saying this: The Book of Deuteronomy, chapter 2, verse 6— again, context. What's going on in this particular Scripture of the Bible is that there are a very talented group of people who have just been released from slavery. So, what God is saying to these people is while you are wandering, trying to find your way, there are a couple of ways that I want you to live and I don't want you to go against these ways. Here's one of them, Deuteronomy 2:6 KJV. My God says to this group of people,

> *"Ye shall buy meat of them for money, that ye may eat; and ye shall also buy water of them for money, that ye may drink."*

Let me break this down. It's so simple, yet so powerful. God is saying to His wandering people, if you don't have the money for the meat, don't buy it. If you don't have the money for the water, don't drink it. I call this my credit card Scripture because you and I are so trapped as a nation that buys, whether we can afford it or not. If we take $2,000 and put it on an 18.9% credit card and we make the minimum payment every single month, the amount of time it would take to pay that off—$2,000, 18.9% interest—the amount of time it would take for us to pay it off making the minimum payments every month: 22 years. By the time we have paid that off, we would have given that credit card company $10,000. That's like saying let me borrow $2,000 and I will give you your money back, plus an $8,000 check. It's time for us to listen to God's words about how we should conduct ourselves while we are wandering and trying to find our way.

The first time I used this statistic, the average credit card balance per person was $958. Today, that same credit card balance is well over $10,000 per person. In January 2009, credit card companies, recognizing that they were struggling, took every 18.9% credit card and upped it to 29.9 and those who did not notice and those who did not argue, they are paying 29.9% on a credit card that used to be 18.9%.

> *"Ye shall buy meat of them for money, that ye may eat; and ye shall also buy water of them for money, that ye may drink."*

Now, I think that the things that I'm sharing are valuable because I'm connecting the way in which we should conduct our finances with the way that God wants us to live. There is one thing about these words that bothers me and that is that everything that I'm saying to you is full of steps, is full of logic, but it's devoid of hope. It does not say, "I hear you, but this is where I am now and how do I get out of the position I'm in?"

Please allow me to share with you one final excerpt from the Word of God: 2 Kings 4:1–7 KJV. Meditate on this passage and know that it's there in 2 Kings, so you'll go to it if you're ever in a spot where you need the hope to get where God wants you to be financially:

> *"Now there cried a woman of the wives of the sons of the prophets unto Elisha, saying, Thy servant my husband is dead; . . .and the creditor is come to take my son. And Elisha said unto her, what shall I do for thee? tell me, what do you have in your house? and she said, I have nothing in my house, save a pot of oil. Go, borrow thee vessels. Take them and give them to your sons. Take these vessels and pour in. When the vessels are full, take the vessels and keep the oil. Then she came and told the man of God. And he said, Go, sell the oil, pay thy debt, and live thou and thy children of the rest."*

Now, let me tell you why I say this passage is so powerful. In the first verse, this young lady is struggling financially and the first thing she does is cry out to the man of God. How many times does someone that we know, instead of crying out to anyone, keep it inside?

It's private. Money is emotional. We don't want to talk about it. In order for her to get through her situation, the first thing she did was to cry out.

In the second verse, he asked her a question, *"What do you have?"* and she said, *"Nothing."* Now, I need you to hear me. She did not say, *"I have a pot of oil."* She said, *"I have nothing, except for a pot of oil."* Now, do I need to remind you that in verse 7 the oil that she said she did not have was the very oil that she used to pay her debt? Hear me. Why is it that when we get into a bad state, we focus on what we don't have? We don't even realize that what we need to get out of our situation is right there. *"What do you have in your house? I have nothing, except for a pot of oil."* How many things are we calling nothing and they're something? How many situations, how many questions are being asked of us and we're saying nothing? We're not focusing on the oil, the anointing to get out of our situations. How many of us are in verse-2 situations right now? We haven't cried out, we're saying nothing.

Verses three through six are important too because in verses three through six, do you know what she's done? She's doing what the man of God told her to do. How many times do we know in our heart that God wants us to take specific action, but we don't do so because we're afraid, because we're focusing on our nothing instead of on our all?

Verse seven, *"Go, sell your oil and pay your debt and live thou for the rest of your life."* How many of us, how many of us know someone who's in a verse-2 situation right now and they're simply four Scriptures away from getting to their verse-7 situation, from getting to their breakthrough? I'd like for you to take this passage and let it resonate with you—you and I have to understand that the principles in these seven verses are so powerful. Cry out, focus on what you have, use your anointing to walk through verses three through six, and you too can be in a situation where you will be in a verse 7 and get out of the very situation that you didn't think you'd be able to get out of.

To be continued. . .

For more on the *The Economic Story of the Hunter and the Lion* visit http://TheHunterAndTheLion.com and follow Brother Dr. Craig Bythewood on Twitter at: http://twitter.com/DrCraigB

Good Success Resource Section

~~~∞~~~

Online Bible Study Websites

- http://BlueLetterBible.org
- http://BibleGateway.com
- http://BibleStudyTools.com

To Register For Your Limited Deluxe Edition Resources, Visit http://LimitedDeluxeEdition.SuccessOnGodsTerms.com or

Scan the QR Code below with your mobile phone: (You may need to download a QR Code reader from your App Store)

Learning More About:

- eLife Ministry
- Business Development
- Home Ownership
- Health and Wellness
- 31 Modes of a Virtuous Woman
- Managing Money God's Way
- And much more plus
- Free mp3 downloads, memberships and eBooks

About the Authors

C. Thomas Gambrell

C. Thomas Gambrell is an eminent speaker, trainer and business success coach. He provides coaching and learning management consulting services to solve training delivery, knowledge transfer and information exchange problems for business owners, member associations, corporations, not-for-profit organizations and public sector clients. As a professional success coach, C. Thomas Gambrell addresses audiences throughout the nation training and inspiring people to become peak performers. Mr. Gambrell's success emanates from a true passion for helping individuals and organizations get more of the right things done in less time.

C. Thomas' captivating messages resonate with a wide variety of audiences because he not only provides inspiration to help others want to be self-motivated, he also shares specific strategies to help them in the achievement of their desired outcomes. Mr. Gambrell offers proven learning strategies and technology solutions that enable organizations to function more effectively in a 21st Century economy.

Mr. Gambrell attended Columbia University where he received a B.A. in Computer Science. Recognized as a consummate professional, C. Thomas has gone through his career achieving at the highest levels. From becoming a corporate trainer and global project manager, to top producing marketing & sales professional, to respected entrepreneur, he is a model of the practical information he shares on thought and performance excellence.

http://CThomasCoaching.com

Gerald D. Rogers

Gerald D. Rogers is a passionate and kingdom-minded author and market place minister. He provides spiritual grounding, physical health and mortgage financing coaching to solve life's challenges for church goers, entrepreneurs and home owners.

Gerald D. Rogers is an advocate for healthy living on all levels. His holistic approach to wellness empowers his clients and audiences with practical information that they can use for their spiritual, physical and economic development. "Success on God's Terms", is the common thread that ties together his inspirational messages about spiritual edification, physical wellness and kingdom building through land acquisition.

Mr. Rogers' championship mindset comes from his days as a collegiate athlete. He completed his education at Florida A&M University where he received a B.S. degree in Criminal Justice and Psychology. In addition to his Criminal Justice career, he has served his community as a mortgage consultant and real estate investor and has helped over 300 families secure their dream of home ownership.

http://HomeOwnershipCoaching.com

If you wish to book the Authors for Book Signings and Engagements, order additional copies of this book or learn about the Success on God's Terms Movement visit us at http://SuccessOnGods Terms.com.

Follow us on Facebook and Twitter at: http://facebook.com/ SuccessOnGodsTerms and http://twitter.com/SOGTTheBook.

CPSIA information can be obtained
at www.ICGtesting.com
Printed in the USA
LVHW091302200820
663727LV00009B/80